MARIA LONGHENA

ANCIENT MEXICO

The History and Culture of the Maya, Aztecs, and Other Pre-Columbian Peoples

STEWART, TABORI & CHANG
NEW YORK

Contents

TEXT
Maria Longhena

EDITORIAL COORDINATION
Fabio Bourbon
Valeria Manferto De Fabianis
Bianca Filippone

TRANSLATION
Neil Frazer Davenport

DESIGN
Patrizia Balocco Lovisetti

GRAPHIC DESIGN
Anna Galliani
Clara Zanotti

DRAWINGS
Monica Falcone
Roberta Vigone

JACKET DESIGN BY
Lisa Vaughn

First published in 1998 by
White Star S.r.l.
Via C. Sassone 22/24,
Vercelli, Italy.

© 1998 White Star S.r.l.

Published in 1998 and
distributed in the U.S. by
Stewart, Tabori and Chang,
a division of U.S. Media
Holdings, Inc.
115 West 18th Street,
New York, NY 10011

Distributed in Canada by
General Publishing Company Ltd.
30 Lesmill Road
Don Mills, Ontario,
Canada M3B 2T6

Library of Congress Catalog
Card Number: 98-84847

ISBN 1-55670-826-2

Printed in Italy

10 9 8 7 6 5 4 3 2 1

(Note: caption
numbers refer to the
pages on which the
illustrations appear.)
Page 1
Menacing heads of the
Feathered Serpent
crown the stairways
of the Platform of the
Eagles, Chichén Itzá.

Pages 2–3
A panoramic view
of the principal
buildings of Palenque,
in the Chiapas region
of Mexico. The Temple
of the Inscriptions is
on the right.

Pages 4–5
A long stone staircase
reaches up to the
summit of the
Pyramid of the Lost
World, at Tikal in
Guatemala.

Pages 6–7
The imposing
Pyramid of the
Magician at Uxmal
has an unusual oval
plan and is composed
of a number of
superimposed
buildings.

Pages 8–9
This beautiful
funerary mask, made
of jade, pyrite, and
shell, comes from
Tikal.

Pages 10–11
A ruined pillared
building precedes the
grandiose Temple of
the Warriors at
Chichén Itzá, in the
Yucatán. The
complex dates from
the period of the
Toltec occupation of
this important Maya
city.

Foreword

by Fabio Bourbon

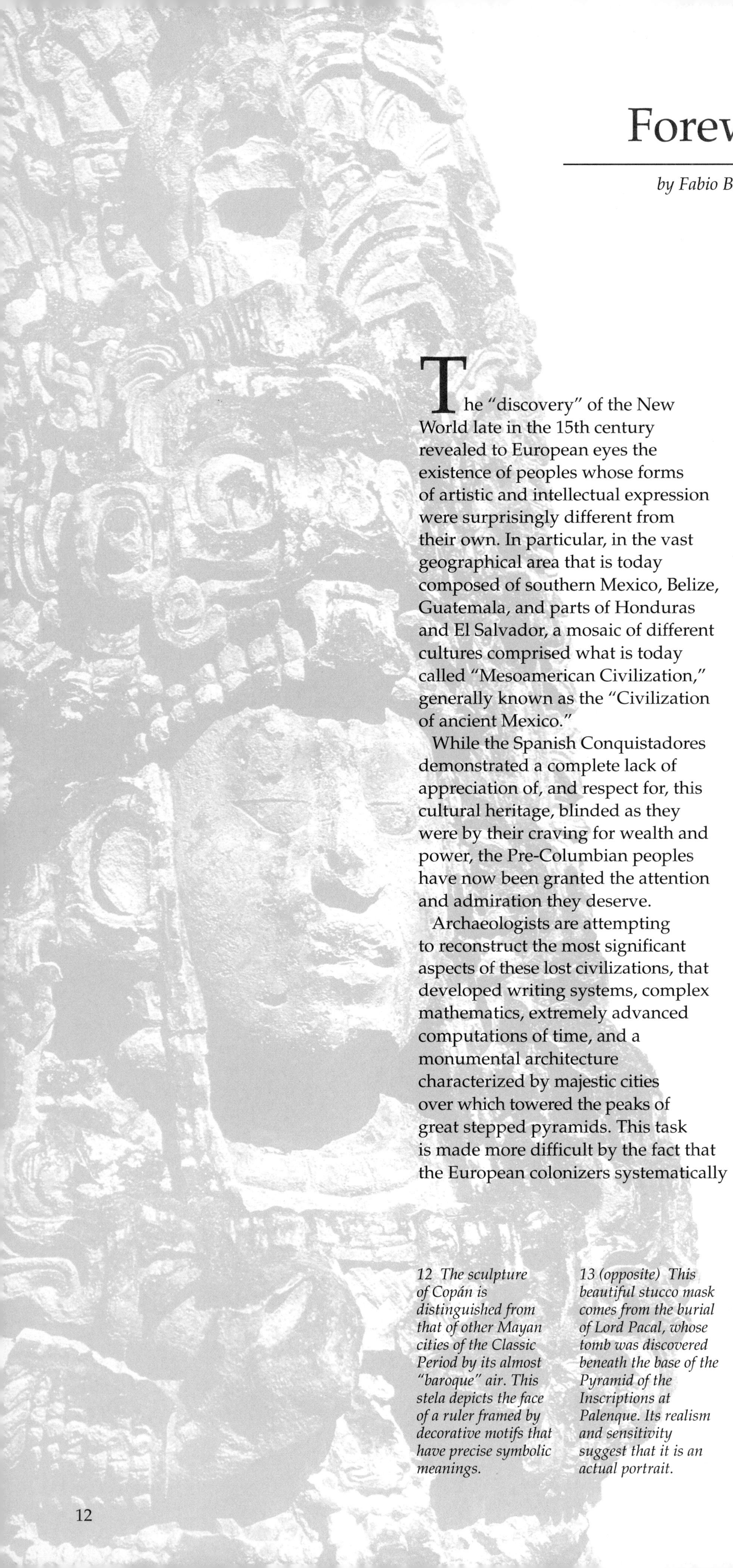

The "discovery" of the New World late in the 15th century revealed to European eyes the existence of peoples whose forms of artistic and intellectual expression were surprisingly different from their own. In particular, in the vast geographical area that is today composed of southern Mexico, Belize, Guatemala, and parts of Honduras and El Salvador, a mosaic of different cultures comprised what is today called "Mesoamerican Civilization," generally known as the "Civilization of ancient Mexico."

While the Spanish Conquistadores demonstrated a complete lack of appreciation of, and respect for, this cultural heritage, blinded as they were by their craving for wealth and power, the Pre-Columbian peoples have now been granted the attention and admiration they deserve.

Archaeologists are attempting to reconstruct the most significant aspects of these lost civilizations, that developed writing systems, complex mathematics, extremely advanced computations of time, and a monumental architecture characterized by majestic cities over which towered the peaks of great stepped pyramids. This task is made more difficult by the fact that the European colonizers systematically attempted to eradicate all traces of these ancient cultures. However, discoveries are continually being made and objects brought to light with increasing frequency that fully justify such interest and further the research.

The aim of this book is to examine the history of a number of these peoples, in particular those who gave rise to the most highly evolved and sophisticated social systems. The Olmecs, Zapotecs, Maya, and Aztecs, have left remarkable testimony of their cultures in the form of great architectural complexes, sculptures, reliefs, ceramics, and jewelry, as well as complex written records that have only recently begun to reveal their secrets. At the same time we will also examine some other, so-called "minor cultures" that up until now have been somewhat overlooked, but which nonetheless contributed to the economic and artistic development of Pre-Columbian Mesoamerica. The text, with accompanying illustrations, provides an accessible and comprehensive overview of the entire historical panorama of the peoples of Central America, from the earliest traces of the Olmec civilization up to the late Post-Classic Period and the arrival of Hernán Cortés—a world of distinctive customs and traditions, and high achievements.

12 The sculpture of Copán is distinguished from that of other Mayan cities of the Classic Period by its almost "baroque" air. This stela depicts the face of a ruler framed by decorative motifs that have precise symbolic meanings.

13 (opposite) This beautiful stucco mask comes from the burial of Lord Pacal, whose tomb was discovered beneath the base of the Pyramid of the Inscriptions at Palenque. Its realism and sensitivity suggest that it is an actual portrait.

14–15 Masks are frequently represented in the art of Teotihuacan. This example, a funerary mask of terra-cotta, dates from the Classic Period and retains traces of its original colored decoration. The large earspools and nose ornament are signs of rank.

16–17 Testimony to the skill of the craftsmen of Teotihuacan in the working of stone, this funerary mask carved from jade is covered with a mosaic of turquoise, pyrite, and shell, and may date to the 8th century AD.

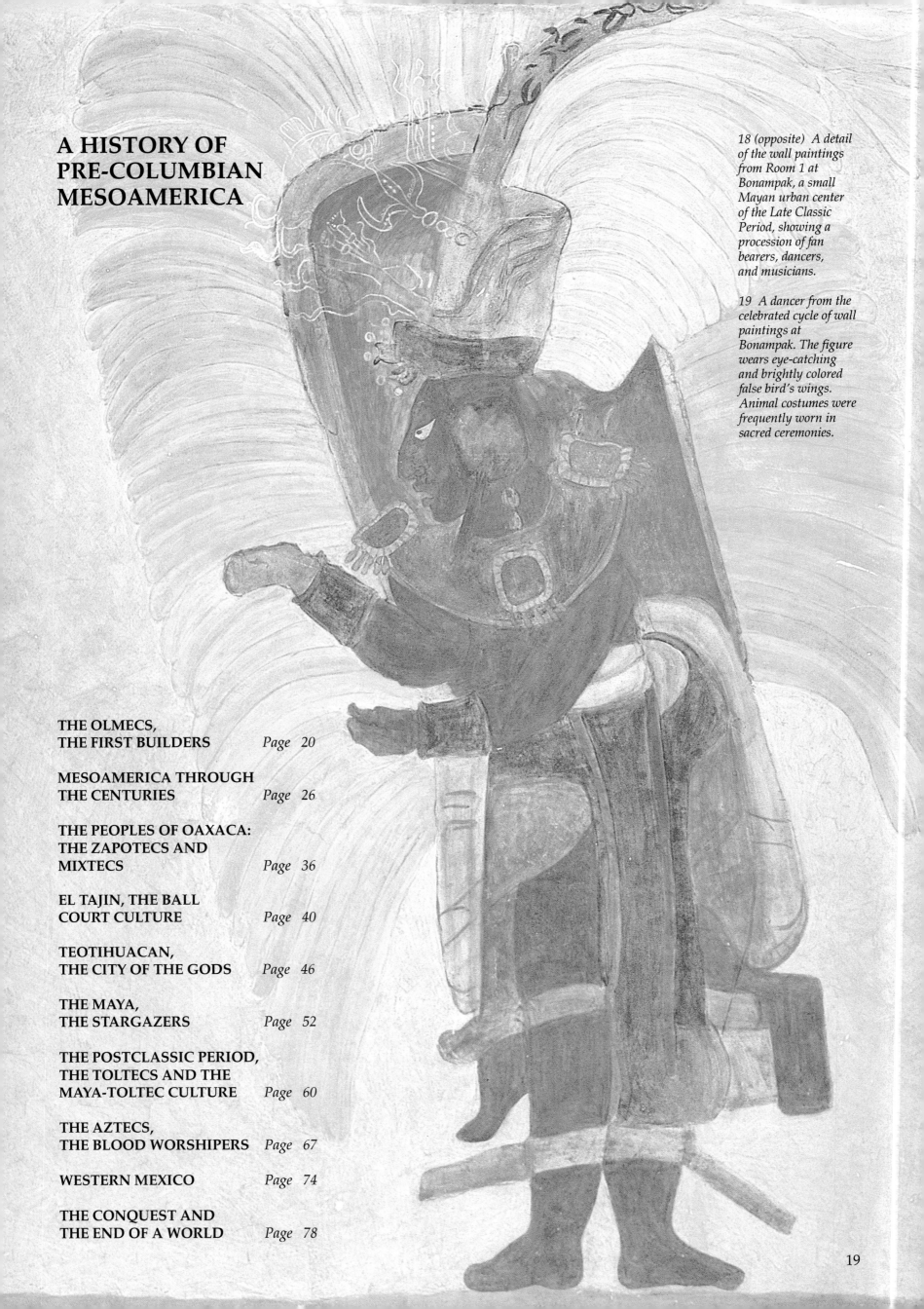

A HISTORY OF PRE-COLUMBIAN MESOAMERICA

18 (opposite) A detail of the wall paintings from Room 1 at Bonampak, a small Mayan urban center of the Late Classic Period, showing a procession of fan bearers, dancers, and musicians.

19 A dancer from the celebrated cycle of wall paintings at Bonampak. The figure wears eye-catching and brightly colored false bird's wings. Animal costumes were frequently worn in sacred ceremonies.

THE OLMECS,
THE FIRST BUILDERS

A Cerro de las Mesas
B Tres Zapotes
C La Venta

The complex mosaic of civilizations that flourished in Mesoamerica from the 2nd millennium BC had its beginnings in the Tropical Lowlands of the coastal band of the Gulf of Mexico. Around 1500 BC this hot, humid region, made fertile by a vast network of rivers and marshes, witnessed the birth of what is considered the "Mother Culture" of ancient Mexico, the Olmec civilization. However, the origins and many aspects of this ancient Mesoamerican culture are still an archaeological enigma. The term "Olmec" derives from Nahuatl, a language spoken by the later Aztecs, and means "Inhabitants of Olmán," that is to say "People of the Land of Rubber." This was how, in the era of the Spanish Conquest, the subjects of Motecuhzoma II described the people living along the coast of the Gulf of Mexico. However, we still do not know the name the Olmec of the 2nd and 1st millennia BC called themselves.

Current archaeological research suggests that the Olmec laid the foundations for the great civilizations and kingdoms, such as those of the Zapotecs, Maya, and Aztecs, that succeeded one another in Central America up to the Spanish Conquest. In order to understand more fully the development and culture of the Olmec civilization it is necessary first to look at the historical and geographical context within which it developed.

Around the 4th millennium BC, following the introduction of agriculture, the first sedentary human groups began to form in Mesoamerica. Maize represented the principal food resource, together with pumpkins and beans. Although certain animal species, such as horse, cattle, and sheep, were unknown in the New World

until the arrival of Europeans, the native people did domesticate dogs and turkeys and exploited bees. While part of their food requirements was provided by agriculture, the ancient inhabitants of Mesoamerica continued to hunt in the tropical forests that were rich in all kinds of birds and game, and fished along the rivers and coasts. During the last centuries of the 2nd millennium BC the fertile territories corresponding to the present-day Mexican states of Veracruz and Tabasco were populated by people living in agricultural villages, many of which were concentrated along the Tonalá and Papaloapán rivers and around the Bay of Campeche.

From around 1200 BC a series of transformations began that can be considered as the embryonic

20 (above) Tlatilco was one of the oldest settlement sites of central Mexico. This acrobat from the site dates to 600 BC.

20 (right) This stone statuette also dates to the Preclassic Period and depicts a wrestler, whose physical features reveal Olmec origins.

21 (opposite) The Olmecs created impressive Colossal Heads in basalt, such as this one from San Lorenzo, Veracruz. It is thought that the Colossal Heads were portraits of high-ranking individuals.

development of a true civilization. At the center of many villages that up until then had consisted of simple huts made of perishable materials, pyramidal platforms of mud and earth were erected to serve as temple buildings, the earliest examples of religious architecture in Mesoamerica. These religious complexes, surrounded by rural villages, are usually described by archaeologists as ceremonial centers, as distinct from the true city which only developed from the first century AD, with the rise of the Maya and Teotihuacan.

The most important Olmec ceremonial centers are San Lorenzo, La Venta, Tres Zapotes, and Laguna de Los Cerros. Archaeological dating demonstrates that San Lorenzo was the first to develop, around 1200 BC, and that, probably around 900 BC, it suffered a violent destruction at about the same time that La Venta began to emerge and flourish.

La Venta, located on an island in the swamps in the heart of the jungle, is now considered to be the largest and most important site in the Olmec cultural area. It was here that the earliest Mesoamerican pyramid structure was erected, measuring 33.8 m (111 ft) high, the conical form of which has been interpreted by some as representing a volcano. These ceremonial centers have yielded various monolithic monuments such as "altars" (probably thrones) and stelae decorated with reliefs, as well as pyramids and platforms. Perhaps the most startling finds from this period are, however, the colossal stone heads weighing several tons, of which 17 are currently known. These gigantic heads, crowned with a form of helmet, have distinctive facial features with almond-shaped eyes, fleshy, down-turned lips, and large flattened noses. These features have prompted scholars to debate the racial origins of the figures represented: although some have seen negroid

22 (opposite) This large greenstone sculpture is known as the "Lord of Las Limas," from the place it was found in the Mexican state of Veracruz. It has been dated to the middle of the Preclassic Period and depicts a young male figure holding an infant in his arms, perhaps the incarnation of the rain deity venerated by the Olmecs.

23 (below) The so-called "baby face" figurines, in stone or terra-cotta, depicting asexual infantile figures with a rounded body, are a very characteristic product of the Olmec people. The figures are usually seated with their legs apart. In this case the figure appears to be rubbing or drying its eyes.

elements in these stony faces, they are generally regarded as depictions of Mesoamerican Indians, many of whom share many facial characteristics. Similar features have also been found in other statues and in reliefs depicting people carrying a child in their arms, and jaguars or jaguar-like beings.

In addition to the great stone monuments, excavations have brought to light smaller objects in votive deposits and the burial assemblages of members of the "elite" that illustrate the sophistication of Olmec artistic expression. These include terra-cotta vessels, terra-cotta figurines with infantile features known as "baby faces," and elegant jewelry and human and zoomorphic figurines carved in jade, serpentine, and obsidian.

Such finds are not restricted to the coastal region of the Gulf, but have also been noted at numerous sites in other regions of Mexico and in Belize, Guatemala, and Honduras. This represents evidence of widespread

Olmec cultural, commercial, and artistic influence that began in 900 BC and continued for several centuries.

Although our knowledge of the origins and history of the Olmecs remains patchy, on the basis of the archaeological evidence and comparisons with succeeding cultures, we can draw certain conclusions and reconstruct, at least in part, some of the main features of Olmec civilization.

At the end of the 2nd millennium BC, within the context of what can be considered as a rural society, a ruling "elite" emerged and established itself: a caste of shaman-rulers who, for the first time in Mesoamerican history, attempted to express their religious and political power through lasting monuments. These rulers may well have wanted to appear in the eyes of the people as the earthly incarnations of deities, and it is presumed that the inhabitants of the villages were obliged to donate regularly a part of their harvests to their rulers, as

23 (above) Another example of a "baby face" sculpture with rather different features: the small hands and feet are painted red, which probably had a ritual significance. The figure is also wearing earrings and a helmet-like hairstyle. Unfortunately, the meaning of much of the iconography of the Olmec culture is still unknown.

well as various offerings. Many scholars believe that the Colossal Heads and statues are portraits of Olmec rulers, who had them carved to celebrate their power. Analysis has shown that the basalt stone used for these works came from the volcanic Tuxtla Mountains, many miles away from the ceremonial centers. The heavy blocks were probably transported by river and over land by rafts, sleds, and wooden rollers.

The Olmec need for jade and obsidian in particular created a trade network along which Olmec religion, the rituals associated with it, and forms of artistic expression may also have traveled to peoples in Mexico and neighboring areas. This laid the foundation of a cultural substratum inherited by later Mesoamerican civilizations, the traces of which survived even the Spanish Conquest.

Olmec religion took the form of a shamanist cult. "Nahualism," a belief that the shaman could transform himself into animal forms, in particular the jaguar, received its name from the later Aztecs, but goes back beyond the Olmec. The *nahual* animals were a kind of alter-ego of the divinities—a fundamental concept that constitutes the basis of the religion of all the peoples of Pre-Columbian America. Shamans communicated with the supernatural world through

24 (below) The group of figurines shown here is part of a funerary cache found at La Venta together with the axe in the previous illustration. Fifteen statuettes in jadeite are turned towards one that is made of grey stone in a deliberate arrangement that is hard to interpret. Perhaps it represents a tribal council or possibly an initiatory rite.

25 (opposite, above) This sophisticated container skillfully depicts a seabird with a long beak. It also comes from the area of Tlatilco.

25 (opposite, below) A variety of vessels in the form of aquatic animals and seabirds have been found at Tlatilco and Las Bocas in central Mexico, perhaps originally intended as censers. This container in grey terra-cotta is from Tlatilco and has been attributed to the Olmec culture.

24 (above) An Olmec votive axe of jade of the middle of the Preclassic Period, found at La Venta. It has the typical features of a monstrous being associated with the supernatural world: the square head has a central cleft, the eyebrows are shown as flames, and the mouth is typical of the jaguar-like beings of Olmec mythology. The arms are folded on the chest in a posture of uncertain meaning.

the use of drugs such as tobacco and hallucinogenic mushrooms that enabled them to achieve a state of ecstasy. Rituals took place in the innermost sanctuaries of temples and in the depths of caves, and were accompanied by sacrifices and autosacrifices. According to one theory the origins of the cult of the jaguar are to be found in the Olmec culture.

Olmec achievements also include astronomical observations related to the study of the planets and the development of calendrical systems, in particular the Long Count, which had great influence on later cultures. The Long Count defined dates beginning from a "year zero." An inscription on a stela from Tres Zapotes includes one of the earliest recorded dates, corresponding to 32 BC. The question of the use of writing is still controversial, and although

some scholars attribute its invention to the Zapotecs, it is possible that a form of glyphic writing was in use towards the end of the Olmec period. Two examples are Stela 1 of La Mojarra and the Tuxtla Statuette. The complexity of Olmec centers, the sophistication and the richness of their religious-cultural elements have prompted many questions regarding the identity of the Olmec people; it is presumed that they spoke a language of the Mixe-Zoquean family.

Following centuries of cultural expansion, the Olmec civilization disappeared around 400 BC, to be replaced by other peoples such as the Zapotecs of Oaxaca and the nascent Maya.

MESOAMERICA THROUGH THE CENTURIES

   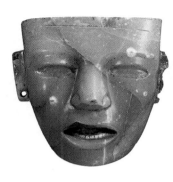 

The Archaic Period
7000–2000 BC

Archaeologists define the period between 7000 and 2000 BC as the "Archaic." During this long period groups of nomadic hunter-gatherers gradually began to cultivate a number of crops including maize, beans, and avocados and to raise animals such as dogs and turkeys. Hunting and fishing were not abandoned, however, and continued to have a significant role in the economy of the peoples of Mesoamerica. The domestication of plants and animals led to a more sedentary lifestyle and from the end of the Archaic Period to the beginning of the Preclassic, the first permanent villages were established, composed of groups of huts built of perishable materials. At the same time religious concepts and cults were developed that, together with material culture, laid the foundations of the future Mesoamerican civilizations.

**Archaic Period
(7000–2000 BC)**

**First settled villages
(2000–1500 BC)**

The Olmecs
1500–200 BC

During the Preclassic (or Formative) Period the Olmecs, the oldest Mesoamerican culture, flourished in the context of the first agricultural settlements. In the tropical lowlands along the Gulf of Mexico the first ceremonial centers were constructed and featured stone religious buildings. A centralized political-religious power structure began to develop in Olmec society and it is from this period that the first traces of shamanic cults and Nahualism date, although their origins are to be found within a more ancient cultural matrix. The Olmecs developed various forms of artistic expression including monumental sculpture and ceramics. The cultural heritage of the Olmecs appears to have influenced all the other Mesoamerican cultures.

**Beginning of the
Preclassic Period
(1500 BC)**

**Development of the
Olmec ceremonial center
of San Lorenzo
(c. 1200 BC)**

**Destruction of
San Lorenzo and
establishment of
La Venta
(c. 900 BC)**

**Beginning of the decline
of Olmec civilization
(c. 400 BC)**

The Zapotecs
600 BC–AD 800

In around 500 BC an important center was established in the Oaxaca region. This was Monte Albán, today considered as the capital of the Zapotecs. This civilization, which in its early stages seems to have been influenced by the Olmec culture, contributed to the development of the Oaxaca region and, almost certainly, to the diffusion of certain cultural features of fundamental importance in the Mesoamerican world: writing, a knowledge of mathematics, and the calendar. Monte Albán enjoyed a period of considerable development above all during the Proto-Classic Period between 200 BC and AD 250, and the Classic Period between AD 250 and 950. Among the most important architectural monuments are the so-called "Building J," perhaps an astronomical observatory, the "Temple of the Danzantes," and numerous tombs of high-ranking figures. The power of the city began to decline from around AD 800 and the role of "capital" of Oaxaca passed to Mitla.

**Presumed foundation
of Monte Albán
(500 BC)**

**Oldest Mesoamerican
calendric inscription
on stone
(around 600 BC)**

**Gradual abandonment
of Monte Albán and the
foundation of Mitla
(AD 800)**

Teotihuacan Culture
AD 200–900

During the late Preclassic Period two centers of great importance rose in central Mexico, Cuicuilco and Teotihuacan. The former was destroyed by a violent volcanic eruption around AD 100. From that moment Teotihuacan took on the dominant role in the region: from a small rural settlement it developed into a true urban center of surprising size, enriched by prestigious religious monuments that were built from around AD 250. Teotihuacan became probably the most important center of the cults of the Great Goddess and the Feathered Serpent. The metropolis was destroyed by fire and was finally abandoned around AD 900.

**Destruction of Cuicuilco
(AD 100)**

**Development of
Teotihuacan
(AD 200)**

**Zenith of Teotihuacan
(around AD 250–700)**

**Final abandonment
of Teotihuacan
(AD 900)**

The El Tajín Civilization
AD 250–900

During the Classic Period (AD 250–900) the most important civilization of the Gulf Coast developed in central Veracruz and its principal ceremonial center was El Tajín. More ball courts have been discovered at El Tajín than anywhere else in Mesoamerica. But many aspects of this culture are still obscure: there is still no certainty even as to the name of the people who lived in the region for many centuries. One suggestion is that they were the Totonacs, who at the end of the Classic Period were replaced by the Huaxtecs. The latter were conquered in turn by the Aztecs.

**Zenith of El Tajín
(AD 600–900)**

**Huaxtec dominion
of El Tajín
(AD 900–1300)**

The Classic Maya
AD 250–950

Maya civilization initially drew on the cultural inheritance of the Olmecs, the Zapotecs, and probably Teotihuacan. Developing these cultural acquisitions from the Proto-Classical Period onward (200 BC–AD 250), the Maya from the highlands erected the ceremonial centers of Izapá and Kaminaljuyú. It was in this geographical region that Maya monumental sculpture, writing, and calendric computation evolved. Subsequently, the Maya civilization of the Classic Period (AD 250–950) flourished in the lowland areas. Ancient ceremonial centers were transformed into powerful and well-organized city states.

The oldest date recorded in a Mayan inscription: AD 292 (Stela 29, Tikal)

Zenith of the Mayan civilization (c. AD 300–800)

Beginning of the decline of the lowland cities (c. AD 800)

Last date recorded in the inscriptions of the lowland regions: AD 909 (Stela of Tonina)

Flourishing of the Puuc style in the Yucatán under the influence of the Putún and Chontal groups (AD 800–1000)

Toltec takeover of the Maya cities of the Yucatán (AD 900)

The Post-Classic Period
AD 950–1500

'At the very beginning of early Post-Classic Period (AD 950–1200) Maya lowland cities were abandoned and fell into decline for reasons still unknown. The centers of the Yucatán enjoyed a period of vigorous development under the cultural and military influence of a new tribal group, the Toltecs. The period also saw great upheavals in other Mesoamerican cultural areas: groups of people from northern Mexico subjugated the cultures that had flourished during the Classic Period, imposing new military regimes and new religious cults. The Toltecs, for example, founded their capital at Tula. Chichén Itzá became the dominant city, a role it maintained until it was overtaken by the city of Mayapán. Weakened by internecine warfare between the groups and rival cities contesting power, the Quiché Maya were definitively conquered by the Spanish invaders at the Battle of Utatlan in 1524.

Early Post-Classic (AD 950–1250)

Fall of Chichén Itzá (AD 1250)

Late Post-Classic (AD 1250–1500)

The Quiché Maya defeated by the Spanish at the Battle of Utatlan (AD 1524)

The Aztecs
AD 1200–1521

Following the invasions by peoples from the northern regions of Mexico, a group of Nahuatl-speaking people took possession of the shores of Lake Texcoco and founded what was to be their capital, Tenochtitlan, on an island. They called themselves "Mexica," but subsequently became known as "Aztec." The name derived from that of the mythical Aztlán, the "White Island," from which according to tradition the new people had originally come. In a short space of time the Aztecs subjugated all the neighboring lands and founded an empire, the enormous power of which was based on a triple alliance of the cities of Tenochtitlan, Texcoco, and Tlacopan. From around 1500, under the rule of Motecuhzoma II, the Aztec empire reached the height of its political and military expansion, but was struck down by the arrival of the Spanish Conquistadores in 1519. Hernán Cortés had Motecuhzoma II killed in 1521: Tenochtitlan and all the subject peoples of the Aztec empire came under Spanish dominion.

Foundation of Tenochtitlan (AD 1345)

Reign of Motecuhzoma II (AD 1502–1520)

Arrival of Cortés in Mexico (AD 1519)

Death of Motecuhzoma II and the annexation of Mexico by the Spanish (AD 1521)

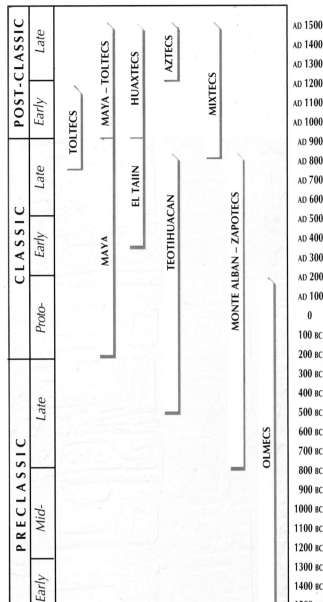

POST-CLASSIC	Late			MAYA – TOLTECS	HUAXTECS	AZTECS	AD 1500
							AD 1400
						MIXTECS	AD 1300
	Early	TOLTECS					AD 1200
							AD 1100
							AD 1000
CLASSIC	Late				EL TAJIN		AD 900
			MAYA				AD 800
						MONTE ALBAN – ZAPOTECS	AD 700
	Early				TEOTIHUACAN		AD 600
							AD 500
							AD 400
							AD 300
	Proto-						AD 200
							AD 100
							0
							100 BC
							200 BC
PRECLASSIC	Late						300 BC
							400 BC
							500 BC
						OLMECS	600 BC
							700 BC
							800 BC
							900 BC
	Mid-						1000 BC
							1100 BC
							1200 BC
							1300 BC
	Early						1400 BC
							1500 BC

THE PEOPLES OF OAXACA:
THE ZAPOTECS AND MIXTECS

Mixtecs **A** Monte Albán
Zapotecs **B** Mitla

36 (below) A terra-cotta figurine from Tomb 113 at Monte Albán, the greatest center of the Zapotec civilization. Its facial features and posture, with the arms and legs outspread, resemble those of Olmec art, but the style is completely different.

36 (right) Numerous stelae were erected by the Zapotec in honor of their rulers and to glorify military enterprises. This stela from Structure E at Monte Albán depicts a figure with the typical attributes of a warrior, including a rectangular shield.

From 600 BC the Oaxaca region of Mexico saw the establishment of a number of ceremonial centers, including Puerto Angel, San José Mogota, Monte Albán, and Monte Negro, the oldest archaeological layers of which reveal the presence of the Olmec culture. However, in the 5th century BC the Olmecs were eclipsed by the growth of other groups, especially the Zapotecs from the Valley of Oaxaca.

At the end of the late Preclassic Period, around 300 BC, the city of Monte Albán took on the role of what today would be defined as the capital of the Zapotec state. The original area was expanded with new buildings including two that stand out for their size and unusual design. The first is the so-called Temple of the Danzantes, named after the 140 figures resembling dancers, but which in fact depict dead captives, carved in relief on slabs on the outside of the base. The second is "Building J," erected at the end of the Preclassic Period, the form of which suggests that it was an astronomical observatory.

Excavations at the great ceremonial center of Monte Albán have formed the basis of reconstructions of the history and culture of the Zapotec. As the Zapotec rulers grew in power and strength up to the Post-Classic Period, Monte Albán was expanded and enriched in terms of art and architecture. Together with religious and ceremonial buildings, the numerous tombs dating from the Classic Period, richly decorated with colorful frescoes, bear witness to the presence of a ruling elite

that held both political and religious power. They ruled a population divided into social classes according to a strict hierarchical system.

Among the tomb assemblages are unusual objects that are characteristic of the Zapotec culture. These are the vessels known as "urns," which resemble funerary urns but which were in fact sacred images and icons.

37 (left) This Zapotec terra-cotta urn depicts a high-ranking figure in a kneeling posture with hands held to his chest. The fine headdress and large earspools are insignia of his rank.

37 (below) Terra-cotta urns with anthropomorphic features and rich polychrome decoration were often placed in the burials of Zapotec nobles. They were not used to contain the ashes of the dead, however, as the name of the object might suggest, because the corpses were inhumed. Rather these elaborate and sophisticated pieces had a ceremonial and votive function. This piece from the site of Las Lomas depicts the Old God, the object of a widespread cult in Mesoamerica.

The Zapotecs were the first Mesoamerican people to use writing in the true sense of the term and to perfect the computation of time and calendrical cycles that the Olmec had possibly already begun to develop. A relief from San José Mogote depicting a dead prisoner is associated with a glyph in the Ritual Calendar of 260 days corresponding to 600 BC, which appears to record his date of birth and is not the year it was inscribed.

Of the glyphs found in Zapotec inscriptions on commemorative stelae, the Temple of the Danzantes, and in tomb paintings, only those with temporal meanings, that is to say calendar dates, and a few place names, have been deciphered. The writing system, therefore, is largely undeciphered, but its underlying structure has been identified, like that of the Maya, as a mixed pictographic-phonetic type. It has been found in regions beyond Oaxaca, including Morelos and Tlaxcala.

Around AD 800 Monte Albán began to decline and there is archaeological evidence of the presence of a different population that infiltrated the area apparently without significant

conflict. These were the Mixtecs, a name meaning "People of the Clouds," whose homeland was in northern and western Oaxaca.

The Mixtecs have left us important historical and iconographical evidence in the form of painted codices covering a period of some 600 years beginning around AD 940. Analysis of the scenes and symbols has enabled scholars, at least in broad terms, to reconstruct historical and dynastic events, and many aspects of the mythology of this apparently warlike people.

38 (top left) The Mixtecs have left us a series of rich tombs. This terrifying object is a white painted ceramic vessel in the form of a human skull sitting on a pedestal.

38 (left) Zaachila was a ceremonial center in Oaxaca that assumed a dominant role in the Postclassic Period, following the decline of Monte Albán. This cylindrical tripod vessel from the site is decorated with a three-dimensional figure representing a human skeleton brandishing two weapons, symbols of war or sacrifice.

38 (right) This unusual Mixtec object also testifies to the importance these people attributed to death and the cult of the deceased. Perhaps a votive urn, it is decorated with a three-dimensional human skull.

Mixtec social and political structure was probably based on the coexistence of small kingdoms, the unification of which was attempted in the 11th century AD by a ruler who has been named 8 Deer. The kingdom he founded, however, disintegrated immediately after his death.

After around AD 900 the Mixtecs dominated the Oaxaca valley, though sites such as Mitla remained Zapotec. In earlier times the Mixtecs had been strongly influenced by contacts with

the Toltecs, but subsequently, from around AD 1200, they developed independently.

Monte Albán was enriched with a large number of tombs. In contrast with those of the earlier Zapotec era, these tombs reveal a change in the cult of the dead with the presence of human sacrifices buried with the dead, and rich funerary assemblages containing jewels and gold vessels.

Mixtec craftsmen were particularly renowned for their skills in goldworking, a craft that until this period was almost unknown in Mesoamerica. Their knowledge of the techniques involved came through contacts with Costa Rica and Panama.

39 (above) To ease their passage to the kingdom of the Underworld the Mixtec dead were buried with numerous objects. This terra-cotta mask, modeled with great skill and precision, has one eye pierced for ritual purposes and scarifications to the face.

39 (left) A graceful blue bird, perhaps a hummingbird, perches lightly on the side of this Mixtec bowl from Zaachila. The shape is simple, but the painted decorations on the surface make it a particularly sophisticated and charming piece.

39 (above) This Mixtec feline head in terra-cotta was once part of a sculpture or container. Particular care was taken to shape the muzzle, the ears, and above all the emphasized fangs. Felines were important in the art and religion of the whole of Mesoamerica until the Post-Classic Period.

EL TAJIN, THE BALL-COURT CULTURE

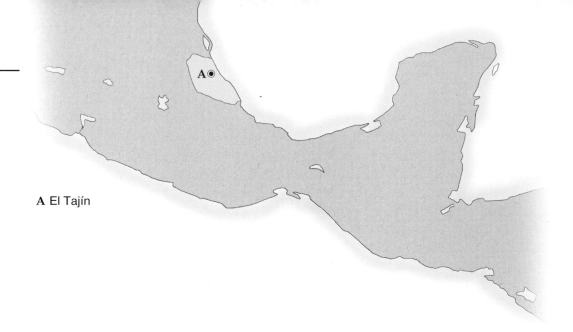

40 (below) During the Classic Period in the Veracruz region, in particular at the site of Remojadas, a distinctive style of pottery production developed. This female terra-cotta statuette with extremely refined and realistic features is one example. As here, the figurines were often elegantly dressed females with their arms extended and mouths open, in an almost smiling or laughing expression. Traces of polychrome decoration are still visible.

During the Classic Period, between AD 250 and 900, a civilization with distinctive features emerged and developed in the geographical area overlooking the Gulf Coast, in particular in the central and northern areas of Veracruz. One of its main centers was El Tajín, a name deriving from a later legend of a local god of storms, Tajín, to whom the city is dedicated. Archaeologists and historians are unsure as to which people the culture of the Veracruz region is to be attributed. Certain factors suggest that it was the Totonacs, an ethnic group that still inhabits the area, but there is no evidence other than the writings of the Spaniard Torquemada that their ancestors had already settled there in the Classic Period. Some archaeologists support this view, while others do not, preferring to talk of the "Veracruz Civilization."

Located in a tropical valley, El Tajín, reached its apogee in the late Classic Period. Archaeological evidence demonstrates that it was not a short-lived occupation as it entered into decline only toward the end of the Post-Classic Period, from AD 1300. The site's most spectacular building, the Pyramid of the Niches, dates to the city's mature period. Around the sides of the pyramid-temple are 365 niches, no doubt linked to the 365 days of the solar calendar. It has been argued that the building was not only a religious temple but also had a precise role in the calculation of time.

Other less impressive temples also have the architectural motif of the niches, together with stylistic elements with origins in Teotihuacan, such as the *talud-tablero* system, consisting of a rectangular flat panel above a sloping wall.

Perhaps the most prominent feature of this mysterious civilization, however, is the ball game. At least 11 ball courts have been discovered at El Tajín, suggesting that this ritual sport had a more significant role here than in other Mesoamerican centers, to the extent that it was transformed into a true cult. Major ceremonial competitions probably took place at El Tajín, attracting participants from surrounding settlements.

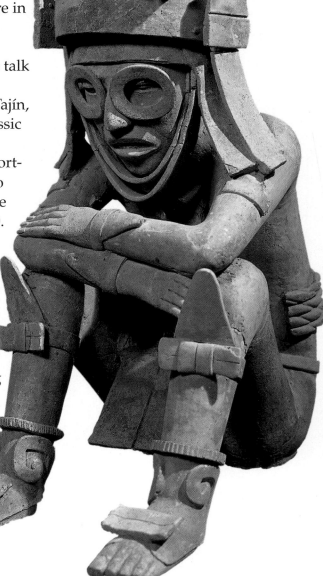

40 (right) This seated figure is one of a series of terra-cotta sculptures from El Zapotral, in the Veracruz region, dating to around AD 700 when the region was possibly inhabited by the Totonac people. The figure is wearing an elaborate head-dress and bizarre rings around its eyes, the significance of which is unknown.

41 (opposite) Dating from the Classic Period, this haunting depiction of a human head in terra-cotta is also from the Veracruz region. Its blank eyes and half-open mouth revealing the teeth perhaps indicate that the subject is dead. The style of representations of male and female figures in the Veracruz region is unlike any other in Mesoamerica.

42 (above) Motifs and objects connected with the ball game are frequently represented in the art of El Tajín. This stone yoke is a reproduction in stone of the protective leather belt worn by the players in the ball court.

42 (below) This Totonac terra-cotta vessel dates from the Classic Period. The shape is very simple while the relief recalls the complex decoration of stone objects of the El Tajín cultural context.

42–43 Together with the "yokes" and the "palmas,"the so-called "axes" or "hachas" were ritual objects that reproduced in stone the actual equipment made of perishable materials used by the players in the ball game. It is thought that the hachas were used as score markers. This one is in the shape of a head—perhaps representing a player. These objects are frequently found in tombs.

Through the ritual ball game the culture of central Veracruz spread throughout Mesoamerica as far as the distant western regions of Mexico. Art objects most closely associated with the ritual ball game are a series of stone sculptures that reached a high level sophistication. These are the so-called "yokes," "*palmas*," and "*hachas*" or "axes," ceremonial objects that reproduced in stone the leather and wooden originals used as equipment in the ball courts. The horseshoe-shaped yokes were replicas of the heavy protective belts worn by the players, the *hachas* were used as score markers, while the elongated *palmas* were perhaps copies of the breastplates inserted in the yokes.

Such objects were produced in great quantities and have been found throughout Mesoamerica. Their symbolic and ritual significance is shown by the extremely elegant decoration, rich in animal and anthropomorphic motifs and fantastic figures, enhanced by complex entwined volutes. Other notable forms of artistic expression of the Veracruz civilization include ceramics, notably the so-called "smiling figurines." Textiles were also important, with a material similar to brocade being developed. The finest wall paintings of this civilization have been found in the burial chambers at the site of Las Higueras.

At the beginning of the Post-Classic Period new cultural factors emerged in the northern part of Veracruz which some have associated with the Huaxtec people. Patchy evidence exists for the presence of these people in the El Tajín region. They were an ethnic group that spoke a Mayan language but developed independent forms of artistic expression from around AD 900. The Huaxtecs have been associated with various circular buildings found in the region that were dedicated to the cult of the Feathered Serpent, suggesting that they had very close contacts with the Toltecs of Tula and Chichén Itzá.

One art form that the Huaxtec excelled in was monolithic sculpture. Generally anthropomorphic, with a rigid, severe structure, these statues usually carried a second figure on their backs: a child or a skeleton. It is thought that these figures represented dual images of the rulers together with their heirs or their ancestors. When the Aztecs extended their dominion to the Huaxtec territory around AD 1400, they almost certainly inherited this stylistic model of stone sculpture.

44 (left) The Huaxtec people emerged in the Veracruz region during the Post-Classic Period. One of their most important art forms was three-dimensional stone sculpture, of which this kneeling figure is an example.

44 (opposite right, above) This Huaxtec sculpture has a rigid and massive three-dimensional form that seems to anticipate the Aztec style. It depicts a deity from the Mexican pantheon, the god Pulque, associated with the figure of the rabbit depicted on his chest.

44 (opposite right, below) Another typical example of Huaxtec art, this sculpture depicts a female figure that has been identified from her pointed headdress resembling a corn cob as Xilonen, the Mexican goddess of young maize.

45 This strange Huaxtec pottery vessel has been identified as either an urn or a censer. It still retains traces of bright polychrome decoration. Its facial features and its ornaments are very unusual and suggest that it was an obscure deity with monstrous features from whose mouth flames seem to emerge.

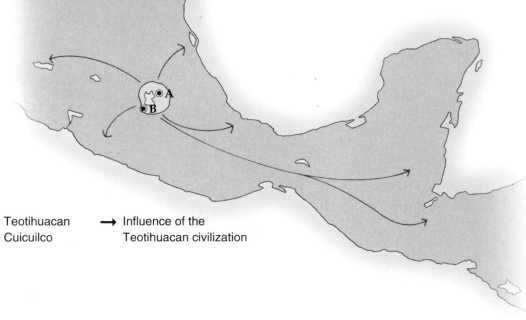

TEOTIHUACAN, THE CITY OF THE GODS

A Teotihuacan   → Influence of the
B Cuicuilco   Teotihuacan civilization

During the late Preclassic Period two central Mexican villages expanded and developed into true ceremonial centers: Cuicuilco and Teotihuacan. Among the ruins of Cuicuilco is a massive stepped platform with a circular base, dressed with stone and equipped with ramps. Archaeological excavations at the site have revealed traces of a violent destruction caused by a volcanic eruption that can be dated to AD 100. The city was completely buried and the surviving inhabitants probably sought refuge at Teotihuacan, the second center in the region, close to Lake Texcoco. Here, the oldest pyramidal platforms were erected later than in Cuicuilco, between AD 200 and 300. These were also dressed with stone but were distinguished by their square bases.

At the beginning of the Classic Period Teotihuacan underwent profound modification and the original small ceremonial center was rapidly transformed into what has been defined as a true "metropolis." Its main arterial route was the extremely long Avenue of the Dead. The city enjoyed its period of greatest splendor around AD 250, when the most prestigious monuments were erected: the Pyramid of the Sun, the

46 A fine example of the sophisticated art of Teotihuacan, this terra-cotta statuette belongs to a group of objects known as "reliquary" or "host" figurines. They depict figures with a strange cavity in the chest within which another figurine is found, perhaps the image of a deity.

47 (opposite) This beautiful censer in painted terra-cotta is from Teotihuacan and dates to around AD 600. The vessel is topped with a cover featuring complicated and colorful decorations in the Teotihuacan style, perhaps representing temple architecture. The iconography is probably linked to the cult of the god Tlaloc.

Pyramid of the Moon, and the Pyramid or Temple of Quetzalcoatl. This last was embellished with abundant sculptural decoration and is one of the most spectacular pieces of architecture in central Mexico.

A series of brick-built houses that can be regarded as true palaces began to replace the original huts made of perishable materials. Between AD 500 and 700 the city reached its maximum extent with a population estimated at around 200,000. A number of old buildings were rebuilt and the housing was grouped in residential districts and subdivided into apartments.

Although numerous outside influences have been recognized at Teotihuacan, the precise identity of the people who built the largest, most flourishing, and most spectacular city of the Mesoamerican world is still debated. Some suggest they were people of Otomí origin, others recognize a Nahuatl-speaking people, perhaps ancestors of the Aztecs, but these are mere hypotheses.

Various cultural factors can be seen in the art of Teotihuacan. The iconography of the Feathered Serpent is very significant; this cult was later spread by the Toltecs in the Post-Classic Period. Further details of the Teotihuacan religion are provided by the magnificent murals that decorate the inner walls of the temples and tombs. One of the most famous is the so-called "Paradise of the Rain God" which depicts in vivid color a spirit kingdom, once thought to relate to the god of rain and fertility, but now the central figure has been identified as a spider goddess.

In addition to their architectural sophistication, demonstrated by certain innovative structural elements such as the *talud-tablero* system, the inhabitants of Teotihuacan also excelled in many other forms of artistic expression: the working of semi-precious stones such as obsidian; weaving; and pottery. Characteristic objects include stone and colorful terra-cotta funerary masks and brightly painted cylindrical tripod vessels.

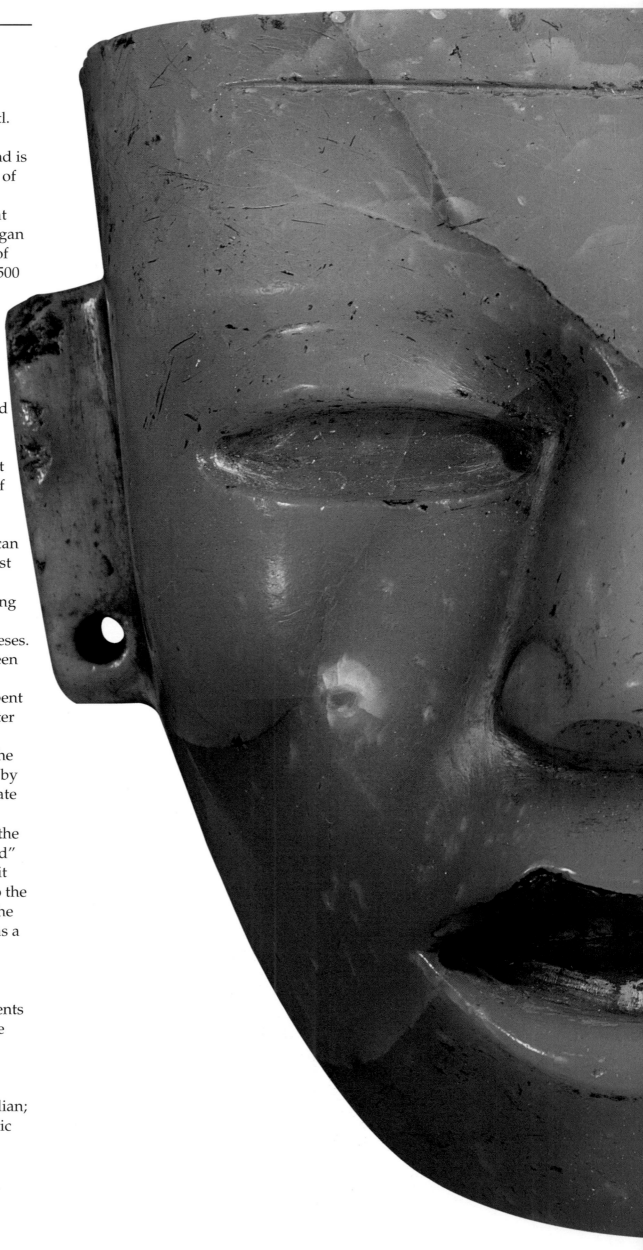

48–49 Among the numerous forms of artistic expression typical of the people of Teotihuacan are funerary masks in various materials. The one shown here is a magnificent example in jadeite: the surviving ear is pierced with a hole from which a pendant earring originally hung. The people of Teotihuacan, like other Mesoamerican peoples, placed masks of precious materials over the faces of deceased nobles, who were buried with other precious jewels. In contrast, members of the more modest classes received a simple disc that was placed in their mouths and acted as an offering for their journey to the Underworld.

Given the extensive distribution of its products, it has been suggested that Teotihuacan was not simply a wealthy metropolis, but that for many centuries it also had a role as a commercial emporium and was an important religious center, the home of the cult of the Great Goddess and perhaps a destination for pilgrims. Merchants and priests, who probably formed the most prestigious social classes, were the main promoters of the spread of the material culture and ideology of Teotihuacan to other peoples, including the Maya.

At some point between AD 650 and 750, Teotihuacan suffered sacking and destruction, possibly at the hands of the Chichimec peoples from the north. The city was definitively abandoned after AD 900, and it is possible that the survivors were responsible for passing on the cult of the Feathered Serpent to the Toltecs of Tula.

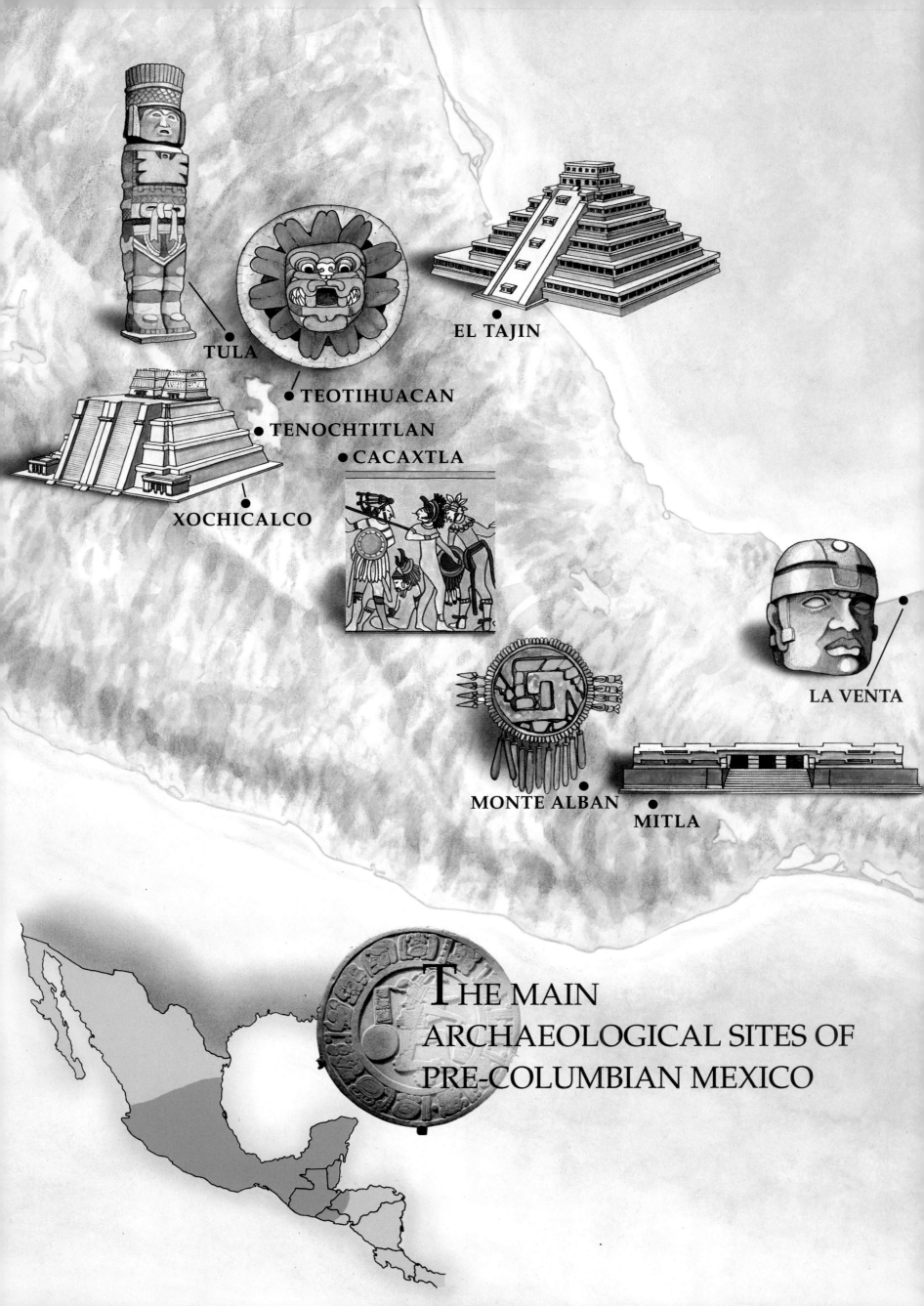

TULA

EL TAJIN

TEOTIHUACAN

TENOCHTITLAN

CACAXTLA

XOCHICALCO

LA VENTA

MONTE ALBAN

MITLA

THE MAIN ARCHAEOLOGICAL SITES OF PRE-COLUMBIAN MEXICO

GULF OF MEXICO

UXMAL

CHICHEN ITZA

JAINA • KABAH

TULUM

• SAYIL

PALENQUE

EL MIRADOR •

UAXACTUN

BONAMPAK

TIKAL

GULF OF
HONDURAS

COPAN

PACIFIC OCEAN

THE MAYA, THE STARGAZERS

The first traces of what centuries later would become the most spectacular and intriguing civilization of Pre-Columbian Mesoamerica, the Maya, date to the late Preclassic Period. In the Chiapas highlands and along the Pacific Coast, beginning around AD 300, a number of villages expanded and developed into larger centers. It is in this context that we find the first evidence of the Maya culture, influenced in part by the Olmec heritage. The most important Preclassic Maya centers were Izapá, El Baúl, and Kaminaljuyú.

Izapá was probably the earliest, with a series of earthen mounds faced with cobbles and stone slabs dating to as early as 800 BC. Izapá is characterized above all by its stone sculpture: stelae and altars with relief decoration featuring iconography related to the religious and cosmogonic concepts that were to become established in following centuries: the Cosmic Tree, an early form of the rain god, Chac, and a number of mythological themes found in the Popol Vuh, the greatest of the Maya sacred texts. Although there are many stylistic similarities between the stelae of Izapá and those of the Olmecs at Tres Zapotes, the former are richer in decoration.

Kaminaljuyú, situated on the edge of modern Guatemala City, developed from around 400 BC. Here, numerous sculptures depicting nobles and rulers, often with divine attributes such as the mask of the bird god, as well as a number of rich burial treasures, bear witness to the success of a ruling caste that enjoyed absolute power combined with a degree of sanctity.

The oldest glyphs and numeric symbols have been found in the earliest Mayan sites in the highlands. This suggests that writing, the study of calendars, and sculpture developed in this geographical region.

52 (opposite) Found in the city of Mayapán, one of the last strongholds of the Maya civilization in the Post-Classic Period. this famous object is a pottery incense burner. It depicts the rain god Chac, or one of his priests.

A	Dzibilchaltún	F	Sayil	K	Tikal
B	Uxmal	G	Edzná	L	Yaxchilán
C	Kabah	H	Palenque	M	Bonampak
D	Labná	I	Piedras Negras	N	Quiriguá
E	Tulum	J	Uaxactún	O	Copán

53 (above left) Also relating to the iconography of the god Chac, this object is made of wood covered with stucco and painted green. It has been dated to the Classic Period and comes from a royal burial cache found in the city of Tikal.

53 (right) A profile view of the incense burner from Mayapán, highlighting the god's long, curling nose. The blue and green colors were associated with the concept of the fertility of water. Incense was used also in later eras in purification rituals.

The ancient lowland Mayan centers have different characteristics: at El Mirador, Cerros, and Uaxactún, stone pyramidal structures were built, with façades embellished by stucco masks depicting the heads of divinities. One lowland architectural development was the false arch, which became widespread in the Classic Period.

For reasons unknown today, some of the centers of the earliest phase of the Mayan civilization, such as Cerros and the important site of El Mirador, were abandoned after just a few centuries of exceptional development. The beginning of the Classic Period, around AD 250, corresponds with the expansion of Mayan centers founded centuries earlier in the tropical lowlands, and the birth of others that reached the height of their power around AD 500. In the midst of the dense jungle vegetation it is still possible to wonder at the ruins that bear witness to the ancient pomp of Tikal, Caracol, Copán, Yaxchilán, Bonampak, Calakmul, and others.

Until around thirty years ago, the history of the Maya was still shrouded in mystery, but with the painstaking study and deciphering of the texts carved on the stone monuments it has been possible to shed considerable light on Maya civilization and to reconstruct its development.

In the Late Preclassic Period villages were transformed: the original rural centers grouped around temples and ceremonial buildings were enlarged into vast complex urban settlements, gradually assuming the status of true cities. Residential quarters, subdivided by broad, paved roads, were built around a central nucleus composed of an acropolis, compounds, plazas, and sacred precincts. Villages continued to exist around the cities, with intensive agriculture as their chief resource.

Tikal was the largest and most densely populated Mayan city, with an urban population of 40,000 and a rural population of around 50,000. Glyphs carved on stelae, temples, and altars form historical texts, narrating tales of the ruling dynasties, their births, coronations, and deeds in war, with each event fixed by a precise date.

In the Classic Period, Mayan civilization expanded into areas of present-day Mexico, Guatemala, Belize, Honduras, and El Salvador. It was not a unified empire, but was composed of dozens of city states, some grouped into confederations. Some experts have interpreted the most recently deciphered texts as suggesting that many of the city states were grouped into two alliances, with Tikal and Calakmul at their heads. Such alliances were probably military in nature and based on the payment of tribute and on diplomatic marriages.

54 (left) Another Maya deity is represented by this large censer: its iconography relates to the Sun God, known to the Maya as Kinich Ahau. The terra-cotta vessel is 1 m (3½ ft) high and was found at the city of Palenque, which flourished during the Classic Period.

55 (opposite) A detail of the face of the censer illustrated left. Traces of the original blue coloring that covered the vessel are clearly visible. The Maya venerated the sun both in its diurnal and nocturnal aspects. At night the Sun God became the Jaguar God of the Underworld.

accompanying texts, exalted their image. They also expanded the ceremonial centers with new ball courts and official buildings.

As well as imposing architectural remains, wall paintings, ceramics and rich funerary treasures, the Maya handed down intellectual discoveries that have led them to be regarded as the pre-eminent civilization of Pre-Columbian America. These discoveries owed much to the Olmec heritage and contacts with other peoples, such as the inhabitants of Teotihuacan and central Veracruz. The Maya excelled in astronomy, the study of calendars, and mathematics. Centuries ahead of the scientists of India they "invented" the concept of zero. In the rare codices that survived the wholesale destruction that followed the arrival of the Spanish Conquistadores, painted images and glyphs illustrate the surprising extent of Mayan knowledge in the fields of astronomy and astrology: daily

Each city was governed by a ruler who held absolute power and was head of the civil administration and probably the priesthood, as well as commander-in-chief of the army. In the eyes of the people, the Maya kings, like the Egyptian pharaohs, embodied an authority and possessed a charisma that were almost divine. They lived in splendor in their courts, surrounded by one or more wives, children, heirs to the throne, and a flock of officials, servants, priests, and artists such as ceramists, weavers, painters, and jewelers. They may also have had slaves—enemies defeated and captured in battle.

Maya society was strictly hierarchical and was subdivided into classes, including craftsmen, merchants, and farmers. Texts have revealed that the Maya were not as peaceful as was once thought. City states frequently fought among themselves, either due to petty rivalry or a desire to expand their territories, or to capture high-ranking prisoners for rites and human sacrifice.

In times of peace the rulers, who included occasional queens, were occupied with increasing the magnificence of their courts and cities. They dedicated temples to the gods, had altars erected, and stelae sculpted with elegant reliefs that, with their events, wars, festivals, and the worship of the gods were linked to the passage of time calculated on the basis of various calendric cycles: the Ritual Calendar of 260 days; the 365-day Civil Calendar; and the Long Count.

The Maya also developed a complex form of writing, with grammar and syntax, that has only recently been deciphered. Thanks to the patient work of a number of Russian, American, and European specialists, it is now possible to reconstruct at least some of the complex mosaic of events, places, dates, and historical figures that make up the history of the Maya civilization.

In the Classic Period religion, organized by an elite priesthood, was still tied to the ancestral shamanic rituals based on nahualism—the manifestation of gods through powerful animals—as well as trances, fasting, and the consumption of hallucinogenic substances. The gods most commonly worshiped were

those linked to agriculture and fertility, such as the Rain God, Chac, and the Maize God. Also of great importance were the Sun God, Moon Goddess, and the creator Itzamná.

Mayan political and cultural power began to decline from around AD 800 to 900, ushering in the Post-Classic Period. Most of the powerful lowland centers were gradually abandoned, with the exception of Seibál, which continued to flourish, probably due to the stimulus of cultural exchanges with Putún people. Commemorative stelae were no longer erected—the latest, discovered at Toniná, bears the date AD 909, marking the end of the ancient ruling dynasties. A great number of hypotheses have been

56 (opposite above) A seated noble receives the homage of another standing figure in this Maya wall relief from the Classic Period. It still retains traces of the bright polychrome decoration used on all the monuments, but which usually does not survive.

56 (opposite below) This Mayan terracotta figurine of the Classic Period portrays a high-ranking figure seated on a throne; his clothing and elaborate headdress are evidence of his rank and position as a member of the court and the noble elite.

57 (above) The Maya were very skilled at working flint and obsidian, often creating bizarre forms known as "eccentric." Some of these may have been scepters. In the example illustrated here the profiles of two graceful human figures can be discerned.

57 (above right) Another painted terracotta censer: the cylindrical vessel is decorated with a face while the cover depicts a monstrous being. This creature is a form of jaguar wearing a loose tunic and can be interpreted as a shaman or priest in the process of being transformed into his animal nahual. Following long rituals the nahual enabled the shamans to communicate directly with the gods.

58 (opposite) In 1952 Mexican archaeologist Alberto Ruz found the tomb of Lord Pacal at Palenque. Among the numerous objects in the sumptuous funerary assemblage of this celebrated ruler were two life-size stucco heads, one of which can be seen here. The heads are thought to be portraits of the dead king and perhaps his wife.

59 (left) This stucco head may also be a portrait of a Maya nobleman. Buried with him as part of his funerary treasure, it was found in the city of Comalcalco and dates from the middle of the Classic Period. Around the head is a kind of band that rulers received on their coronation.

59 (below) Found at Villahermosa, this incense burner is an example of Classic Period Maya pottery. A polychrome terra-cotta figure in a solemn posture, perhaps a priest, is set in a complex frame of volute motifs which could be described as "baroque."

formulated to account for the collapse, or more precisely, the decline of Maya civilization after centuries of splendor. However, the matter has still to be satisfactorily explained. In all probability there was no single cause, but rather a series of cumulative factors. It has been suggested that a succession of poor harvests caused food shortages, population decline, and the interruption of trade links. This coincided with dynastic squabbles and increasingly violent conflicts between city states struggling for territorial domination. Such factors perhaps undermined the foundations of the Maya political system and brought about its fall. Although the lowlands were abandoned, Maya civilization was not extinguished as new cities flourished in the region of Yucatán: buildings at Uxmal, Sayil, and Labná are sophisticated examples of the architectural style known as Puuc that flourished in the region south of the modern city of Mérida.

From around AD 1000 the city of Chichén Itzá expanded and was a kind of capital of the last bastion of the Maya. The development of the Yucatán centers, however, took place under the military and cultural influence of a people from the north, the Toltecs.

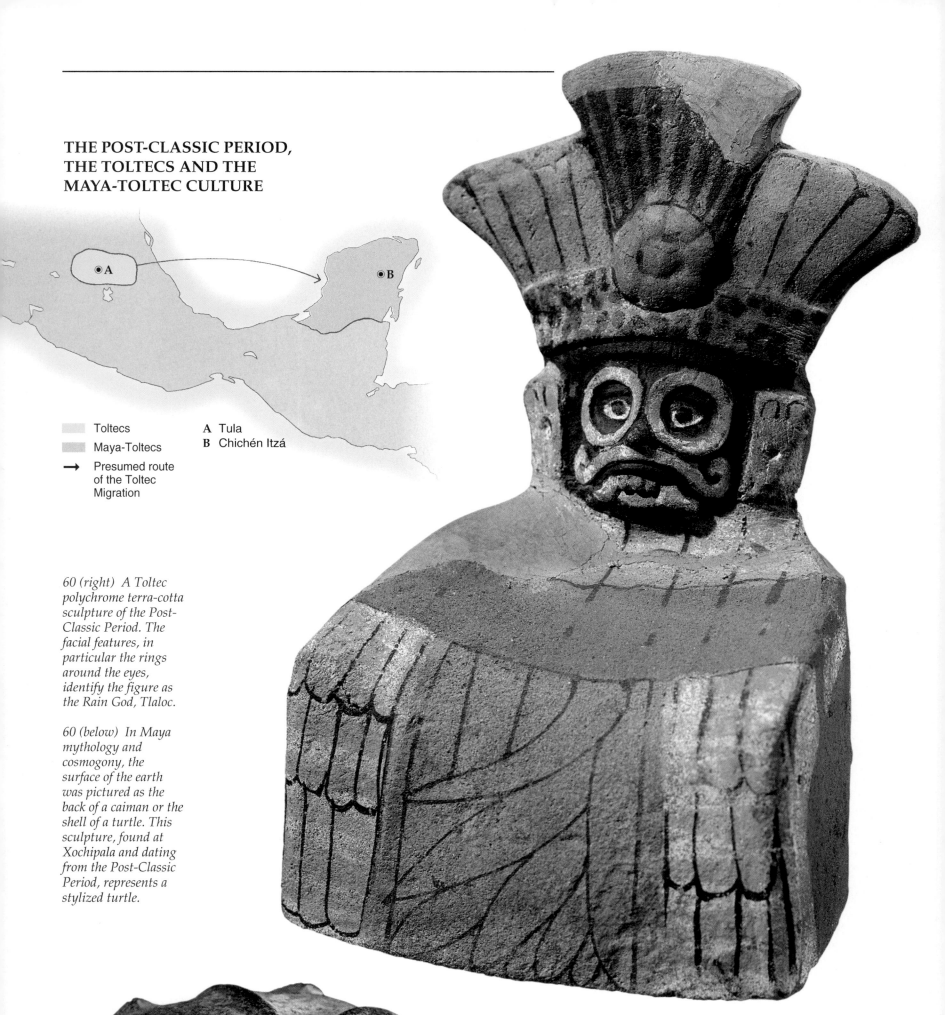

THE POST-CLASSIC PERIOD, THE TOLTECS AND THE MAYA-TOLTEC CULTURE

Toltecs

Maya-Toltecs

→ Presumed route of the Toltec Migration

A Tula
B Chichén Itzá

60 (right) A Toltec polychrome terra-cotta sculpture of the Post-Classic Period. The facial features, in particular the rings around the eyes, identify the figure as the Rain God, Tlaloc.

60 (below) In Maya mythology and cosmogony, the surface of the earth was pictured as the back of a caiman or the shell of a turtle. This sculpture, found at Xochipala and dating from the Post-Classic Period, represents a stylized turtle.

61 (opposite below left) The form and style of this strange Toltec vessel seem much simpler and less sophisticated than Maya pottery of the Classic Period. It depicts a dog with a rope around its neck.

61 (opposite, right above) The relief decoration of this small cylindrical container recalls ancient religious motifs passed down from the Maya to the Toltec civilization. A figure with cat-like teeth and rings around its eyes holds a scepter in the form of a serpent in its hand.

61 (opposite, right below) Two high-ranking figures, one of whom is bearded, are involved in a heated discussion on this attractive Toltec ceramic tankard. Here, elaborate relief decoration is combined with a simple form. Their bird headdresses are portrayed in great detail.

In the centuries immediately preceding the Spanish Conquest, the Toltecs filled the power vacuum in Mesoamerica. Shrouded in legend, stories of their origins and deeds, shifting between history and myth, were still handed down from generation to generation among the peoples of Yucatán in the 18th century.

Around the year AD 950 a period of ethnic and cultural upheaval began that saw the decline and eventual disappearance of a number of great civilizations. Known as the Post-Classic, this period represents the last phase of the Pre-Columbian cultures of Mesoamerica. One element of these upheavals were migrations of groups of people of Nahua stock who arrived from the north, that is, from beyond northern Mexico. The Aztecs called

them the Chichimecs, which in Nahuatl means "The Dog People." In written and oral tradition they were defined as "barbarians" because they founded no cities, had a warlike temper, and fought with weapons such as bows and arrows unknown until then in Mesoamerica.

Documents written after the Spanish Conquest in the Nahuatl language but using the Roman alphabet contain information about the history of the Chichimecs and related peoples. Often the traditions recorded are contradictory, and the most reliable are considered to be those contained in the Annales di Cuauhtitlan. These relate how in AD 950 Chichimec barbarians invaded Mexico's central plateau under the leadership of an adventurer named Mixcoatl ce Tecpatl, meaning

"A Sacrificial Knife." After subduing the local peoples and many cities, including Xochicalco and Cholula, he chose Colhuacan on the eastern shore of Lake Texcoco as his capital. Here he married a princess and had a son, Topiltzin, born in the year 1 Reed. It is around this legendary, or possibly even historical, figure that the history and traditions of the Post-Classic Period revolve. He became a priest of the god Quetzalcoatl, the Feathered Serpent of Teotihuacan origins, and, at the end of the 10th century, founded a new capital in the plains of central Mexico, called Tollan, subsequently renamed Tula by the Spanish. His people, followers and subjects of Quetzalcoatl, were named the Toltecs, from the Nahuatl Toltecatl, meaning "excellent artist." Historically, the Toltec civilization can be seen as a great unifying force. At the height of its power, Toltec dominion extended throughout western Mexico, Yucatán, and Oaxaca, after having absorbed the survivors of Teotihuacan.

The ruins of Tula, in the modern state of Hidalgo, have been described as representing a city with magnificent tall buildings, but in reality they reflect a city of modest size where typical Mesoamerican features, such as the ball court, are found alongside newer elements such as the sacrificial altar, the chacmool. Toltec religious iconography seems to be imbued with elements from Teotihuacan—primarily linked to the Feathered Serpent.

On the basis of oral traditions and archaeological evidence we can reconstruct an overview of the spread of Toltec groups from Tula. Around AD 1000, following sporadic cultural contacts with the Maya population of Yucatán, the Toltecs became the dominant force in the area. At this point the site of Chichén Itzá took on a pre-eminent role and became the largest and most powerful city in Mesoamerica. As a result of these developments, the last Maya bastion in the Yucatán has been called the Maya-Toltec civilization.

At Chichén Itzá above all, but also at other sites, new architectural and iconographical elements were introduced, merging with those of the existing lowland culture. Some gods of the Maya pantheon were supplanted by a new cult that was spread rapidly through Mexico by the Toltecs—the cult of Quetzalcoatl, a Nahuatl word meaning the "serpent with quetzal plumes." Called Kukulcan by the Maya, the iconography of this god prevailed over that of other ancient deities venerated in the Classic Period.

62 (above) The ball game had ancient origins and was played up to the Spanish Conquest. This stone object carved in the shape of a stylized parrot's head was used as a score marker. It is from Xochicalco, a city that flourished after the fall of Teotihuacan.

62 (center) Toltec art, generally severe and simple in form, was occasionally more complex and sophisticated, as demonstrated by this sculpture covered with mother-of-pearl scales. It depicts a figure, perhaps Topiltzin Quetzalcoatl himself, wearing an animal headdress, thought to be the Feathered Serpent by some but a coyote by others.

62 (right) The Toltecs introduced some forms of artistic expression associated with rituals and customs unknown to the Maya of the Classic Period. The chacmool, carved from stone and perhaps a sacrificial altar, was shaped as a reclining man with his back raised, legs folded, and head turned to one side, like this example from Tula.

63 (opposite) The so-called "Stone of the Four Glyphs," found at Xochicalco, is a calendrical stela. On one side are four glyphs relating to dates: 5 Reed, 4 Rabbit, 7 Reptile's eye, 6 A.

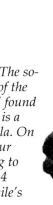

Two legends, as complex as they are fascinating, revolve around the fate of this divine priest-king, founder of the Toltec empire. Topiltzin Quetzalcoatl was seen as a sort of prophet who came to Tula bringing all forms of knowledge in the fields of art and science. When he was forced to leave the city by the evil trickster Tezcatlipoca, he journeyed to the Atlantic coast where, as one legend tells, he ascended into the heavens, transforming himself into the Morning Star (Venus).

A variation of this legend, on the other hand, describes how, after having abandoned Tula, Topiltzin Quetzalcoatl embarked on a raft of serpents and sailed toward the east. When he reached the Yucatán he colonized the region, bringing new knowledge to the people of Chichén Itzá. Between the lines of these mysterious legends concerning the figure of Quetzalcoatl-Kukulcan can be read the story of the invasion and conquest of the Maya Yucatán cities by the aggressive Toltecs.

At Chichén Itzá, alongside the iconography of the Feathered Serpent, there is evidence of another new religious practice. This is the cult of the Sacred Cenote, the well dedicated to the Rain God Chac. Numerous victims were sacrificed by throwing them into the well, where they drowned in the deep, murky waters.

Architectural and sculptural innovations found at Maya sites of the Post-Classic Period reveal a militaristic power. In contrast with the Maya rulers, however, the warrior kings from Mexico did not exalt their own prestige through representations of themselves or their dynasties—at least no such iconography or inscriptions have been recognized.

A number of sacrificial rituals not commonly practiced in the Classic Period, such as the tearing out of living human hearts, took place on a large scale under Toltec dominion. The still beating hearts of the victims may have been placed on the chacmool sculptures. Another introduction linked to human sacrifice was the *tzompantli*, a wooden rack, of which stone copies survive, used to display decapitated skulls of enemies or defeated ball game contestants.

After around AD 1200, the powerful cities of Tula and Chichén Itzá entered into a slow decline. The dominant role in Yucatán was taken over by Mayapán, a fortified citadel, under a lineage named Cocom. Shortly before the European Conquest, a revolt led by another group, the Xiu, destroyed Mayapán and the site was abandoned.

64 (below) This stiff, rather block-like sculpture is one of the supports of a platform for a throne in the Temple of the Warriors at Chichén Itzá. It can be dated to a period between the 11th and the 12th centuries AD.

64 (above) A pyrite mirror may once have occupied the center of this disc, made of wood covered with a mosaic of turquoise and coral featuring a serpentine motif. It is perhaps one of the most sophisticated objects of Maya-Toltec art.

65 (opposite) The Toltecs introduced several new artistic and architectural elements at Chichén Itzá. Among these, human heads emerging from the jaws of animals were very frequent. The symbolism of such sculptures is undoubtedly linked to bloody rituals such as decapitations and human sacrifice.

When the first Spaniards landed on the coast of Mexico and began to explore the land, Motecuhzoma II's Aztec empire was at the height of its power. In contrast, almost all the ancient Maya and Toltec cities lay in ruins, surrounded by villages whose inhabitants still made pilgrimages to the Sacred Cenote of Chichén Itzá. They preserved precious documents, known as codices, that contained the secrets, science, and religion of their Maya ancestors. Almost all the codices were burned by the Conquistadores, who believed them to be the work of the devil. Very few survived, and irreplaceable information recorded by the ancient scribes was lost due to this wanton destruction. In the highlands, in 1524, the Spanish struck an alliance with the Cakchiquél city of Iximché and inflicted a definitive defeat on the Quiché Maya at Utatlán. In the course of the following century the ancient sacred texts known as the Popol Vuh and the Books of Chilám Balám that dealt with Maya prophecies and creation myths were transcribed in the Roman alphabet. These texts, along with the four codices found to date have shed some light on the ideology, cults, cosmogony, and astronomy that were the heritage of the Maya.

A Tenochtitlan/
Tlatelolco

A

67 (bottom) Aztec
history was also
recorded by some
Spanish chroniclers in
the Colonial era. The
page shown here is
from the Historia de
las Indias, *written in*
1579 by Diego de
Durán, depicting the
construction of
Tenochtitlan.

THE AZTECS,
THE BLOOD WORSHIPERS

The Aztecs represent the last great
empire in Pre-Columbian Mexico prior
to the Spanish Conquest and
colonization. Their origins, like those
of the Toltecs, are surrounded with
myths and legends. According to the
chronicles, a Nahuatl-speaking people,
probably the last Chichimecs who
migrated from the north, settled on the
shores of Lake Texcoco. These people
called themselves "Mexica" and the
name they gave to the city they built
was Mexico Tenochtitlan, later
shortened to Tenochtitlan and then to
Mexico by the Spanish. One of the
legends of the Mexica told of an
imaginary place called Chicomotzóc or
"Place of the Seven Caves." Another
enigmatic story relates how the Mexica
reached the country after a lengthy
period of wandering from their
original home known as Aztlán, which
means "White Island" and gives the
root of the word Aztec, the name the
Europeans used for them.

66 (opposite) The
Aztecs created well
organized, highly
trained armies of the
fiercest warriors for
conducting wars not
only with expansionist
aims, but also to
acquire enemy captives
for sacrifice to the
gods. The Aztec army
was divided into
societies or orders: this
terra-cotta sculpture
from Tenochtitlan
depicts an eagle
warrior.

67 (above) Aztec
history and thought
have been handed
down to us in their
codices: this page from
the Codex Boturini
illustrates a stage in
the lengthy Aztec
migrations.

67 (above right) The
opening page of the
Codex Mendoza
depicts the legend of
the foundation of the
Aztec capital,
Tenochtitlan.

68–69 The Aztecs excelled in working stone. This basalt slab reveals a surprisingly sophisticated style: set within a frame of geometric motifs an eagle perches on a plant and devours a serpent.

69 (opposite above) Along with the eagle and the jaguar, the coyote was one of the totemic animals of the Aztecs. This coyote covered with flames or feathers is another example of Aztec skill in stone sculpture.

If, as is often the case, the legend has a core of historical truth, the original homeland of the Mexica was probably a distant island. According to some traditional stories, after they had entered Mexico, the Aztecs eventually reached Tula where they acquired useful knowledge, enhancing their civilization. The arrival at Tula is perhaps a metaphorical representation of the passage from a nomadic to a sedentary lifestyle, possibly as a result of contacts with the remnants of the

Toltec people. The destination towards which the Mexica were moving was, however, Lake Texcoco. Here, the priests laid the image of their tribal god Huitzilopochtli. After numerous vicissitudes and territorial struggles with neighboring tribes, in particular the warlike Tepanecs, and following a sign sent by the gods, the Mexica people founded their capital on a number of swampy islands and named it Tenochtitlan after the leader Tenoch. Tradition has it that some

1428 and from that point on pursued a vigorously expansionist policy that had a dual purpose. One aim was the opening of new trade routes and the collection of tribute, firstly from neighboring peoples and then from ever further afield, along the Gulf Coast and in the Veracruz region.

Within Aztec society a group known as *pochteca* consisted of merchants who covered huge distances to acquire luxury goods, thus promoting the policy of economic and military expansion that enabled the people of Lake Texcoco to lay the foundations of a future empire.

Over the years the Aztecs expanded their religious pantheon, adopting new divinities and the traditional cults of peoples they subdued and forced to pay tribute. However, they directed their principal devotions to Huitzilopochtli, the warrior god of the sun and the ancestral tribal divinity, of whom no representations exist.

In the sacred precinct in Tenochtitlan the Aztecs erected a great pyramidal temple that the Spaniards named the Templo Mayor. The principal façade of this temple rested on a vast platform facing west; two staircases led to the upper level on which were dual sanctuaries. That to the south was dedicated to Huitzilopochtli and that to the north to the Rain God Tlaloc, worshiped throughout Mesoamerica from the earliest times. Archaeological research has revealed that this

69 (below) This square stone seat has a decorative motif with a precise meaning associated with the Aztec calendar. The animal carved in low relief in the centre is a rabbit and refers to a date, the year "1 Rabbit," which corresponds to 1480 in our calendar. Aztec years were designated by four glyphs: "Home," "Rabbit," "Reed," and "Flint Knife."

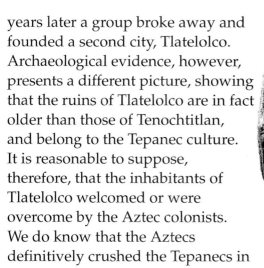

years later a group broke away and founded a second city, Tlatelolco. Archaeological evidence, however, presents a different picture, showing that the ruins of Tlatelolco are in fact older than those of Tenochtitlan, and belong to the Tepanec culture. It is reasonable to suppose, therefore, that the inhabitants of Tlatelolco welcomed or were overcome by the Aztec colonists. We do know that the Aztecs definitively crushed the Tepanecs in

Xochiyaotl in Nahuatl. These were wars undertaken not for conquest but were arranged conflicts designed to capture the greatest number of human victims who would be sacrificed to feed the god with their blood.

A series of rulers of Tenochtitlan maintained the policies of expansion and religious and political repression; when, in 1502, the last independent Aztec king Motecuhzoma II came to the throne, the empire had grown to vast dimensions and included most of central Mexico and reached to the border of Guatemala. Tenochtitlan had not held absolute sway until this time, however, as a few decades earlier it

had entered a "Triple Alliance" with two other principal centers of the region, Texcoco and Tlacopan. Until the early 16th century, therefore, rather than an empire under the rule of a single monarch, a confederation of allied cities existed, to whom subject states paid tribute. There were also military outposts that were not true colonies but were rather buffer-states who, in return for being exempt from paying tribute, provided military defense for the frontiers. Tenochtitlan was, however, pre-eminent: its rulers received the highest proportion of the tribute paid and it was there that the principal religious sites were located.

70 (left) One of the most famous images of ancient Mexico and one of the emblems of the Aztec civilization, the Sun Stone has the face of the sun, or perhaps the "Earth Monster" carved in the center. Around the face are the symbols of the 20 days of the Ritual Calendar, though the stone is not a functioning calendar.

principal Aztec religious center was rebuilt seven times: the two sanctuaries brought to light by meticulous excavation are labeled "Stage II," and date from 1390.

One of the cults adopted by the Aztecs was that of Xipe-Totec which literally means "Our Flayed Lord," a god originating in Guerrero and subsequently borrowed by the Mixtecs as the god of goldsmiths.

Other deities in the Aztec pantheon frequently represented include Tezcatlipoca, "Smoking Mirror," who was associated with destiny and fate; Coatlicue, goddess of the earth and fertility; Mictlantecuhtli, lord of the land of the dead; and Mayahuel, patroness of the maguey agave and *pulque*, an alcoholic drink made from it. Aztec religious practices soon took on an imperious and authoritarian aspect toward the people they dominated who were forced to venerate Huitzilopochtli and take part in human sacrifices in his honor. Moreover, many idols venerated by these peoples were removed from their sanctuaries and locked away in a kind of "prison of the gods," a building in Tenochtitlan called *Coateocalli.* Another blood-curdling aspect of the cult of Huitzilopochtli was the so-called "Flower Wars," or

70 (top) The Aztecs recorded their history and the story of their arrival in Mexico in pictorial codices in which history and legend are combined. Stone was, however, also used as a means of celebrating the enterprises of the Aztec sovereigns: this commemorative stela was carved in honor of King Tizoc and his victories.

This situation did not satisfy Motecuhzoma II's desire for absolute rule and he overturned the Triple Alliance, concentrating power in his own hands. Texcoco and Tlacopan were relegated to a subordinate role and Motecuhzoma launched a campaign of conquest against those people who had yet to be annexed, including the Mixtecs of Oaxaca and the Yopi of Guerrero. The frontiers were also consolidated and rebellious states subdued. At the same time

Motecuhzoma set about making Tenochtitlan the most elegant and sophisticated of the major cities. Founded on the swampy islands of Lake Texcoco, it was transformed into a fabulous and impressive city, built around a network of canals and rich in gardens, zoos with animals and birds of all kinds, magnificent palaces, private buildings, and pyramid-temples. A great stone aqueduct supplied the city with drinking water from sources in the Chapultepec hills.

70 (opposite below) This human head carved from stone could equally be a portrait of a king or an ordinary citizen. It is an example of artistic expression charged with realism. The half-open mouth reveals a row of white teeth made with pieces of shell, while the eyes are inlaid with shell and pyrite.

71 (above) The Stone of Tizoc has a solar disk carved on its upper face. Around the edge is a relief depicting the king victorious against various deities who represent the respective enemy towns. This piece carries the calendar date "8 Reed" which corresponds to the year 1487 of our calendar.

71

By the time of the Spanish Conquest this metropolis boasted a population of over 200,000. Motecuhzoma lived in an immense palace built next to the Templo Mayor, surrounded by a court of concubines, dignitaries, servants, and slaves. The ordinary people, *macehualtin*, were divided into groups or clans, *calpolli*, each of which had its own leader. Members of a *calpolli* worked their own land, retaining part of the produce and handing over the rest to the king in tribute. Certain quarters of the city were reserved for foreigners, many of whom worked as craftsmen. Among these the Mixtecs enjoyed great respect for their skills as goldsmiths and jewelers. Products were displayed and sold at Tlatelolco which, having been reduced to a suburb of the capital, was effectively one huge market. The most precious goods were gold and turquoise, ceramics, stone mosaics, and feathers. Like the Inca of Peru, the Aztecs were great borrowers and adapters of artistic and craft expression from the people they conquered.

Today, with the partial exception of the Templo Mayor, the remains of the ancient city of Tenochtitlan do not do full justice to its original splendor and vastness as described by the Spanish chroniclers. What has survived best is stone sculpture, perhaps the most original form of Aztec art. Usually taking as its theme religious iconography, it is imbued with great strength and expressive power.

Probably the most famous piece of sculpture is the so-called "Sun Stone," a gigantic disk decorated with a complex symbolism relating to the calendars inherited from the older Mesoamerican cultures and used by the Aztecs. Many documents were also written and painted that have survived the Conquest much better than those of the Maya. The system of writing, similar to and perhaps derived from the Mixtecs, has recently begun to reveal its secrets.

At the height of its power the Aztec empire fell to the Conquistadores. The Spanish army that landed in Mexico in 1519 under the leadership of Hernán Cortés was welcomed with reverence by Motecuhzoma II, who identified the light-skinned, bearded foreigners as messengers of the god Quetzalcoatl. After two years of fighting, Cortés destroyed Tenochtitlan. The population was almost annihilated and not even Motecuhzoma was able to escape his sad fate. The survivors

were forced to convert to the Catholic religion and to accept the authority of the Spanish crown. The Mexica empire ceased to exist as such and became a colony known as New Spain.

We have two sources that enable us to reconstruct the history, religion, and daily life of the Aztecs: the Nahuatl pictographic codices saved from the general destruction and the "chronicles," manuscript accounts compiled by Spanish missionaries of the Colonial period.

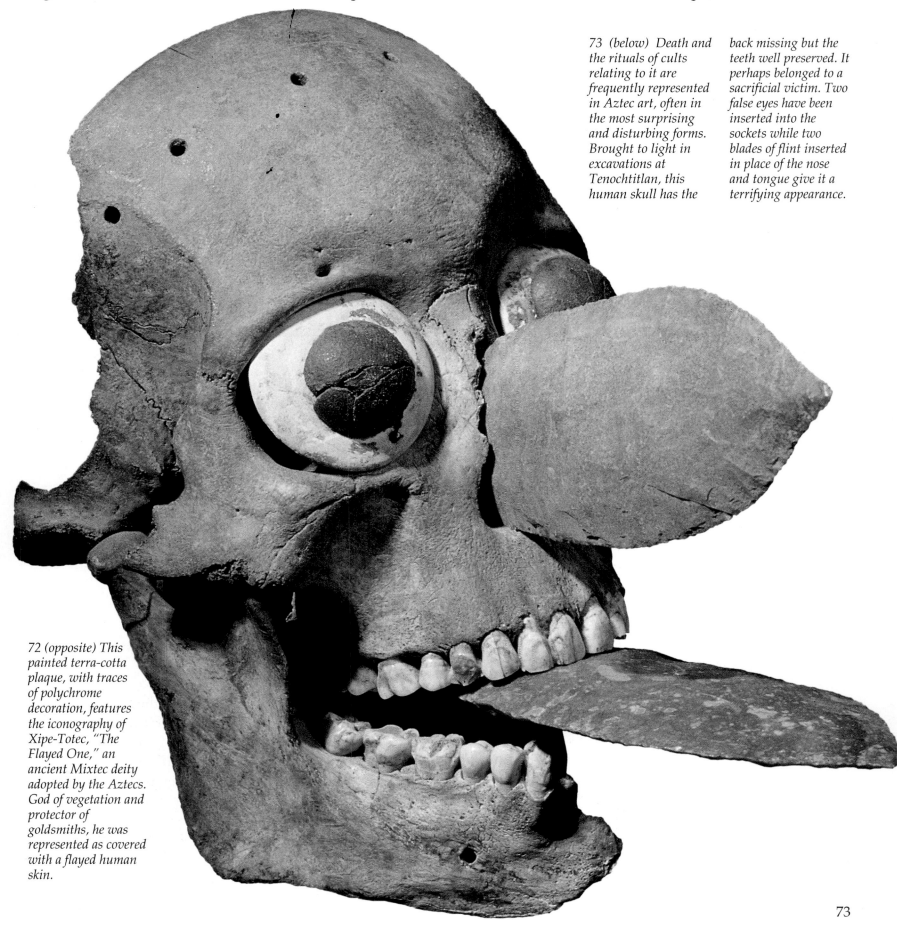

73 (below) Death and the rituals of cults relating to it are frequently represented in Aztec art, often in the most surprising and disturbing forms. Brought to light in excavations at Tenochtitlan, this human skull has the back missing but the teeth well preserved. It perhaps belonged to a sacrificial victim. Two false eyes have been inserted into the sockets while two blades of flint inserted in place of the nose and tongue give it a terrifying appearance.

72 (opposite) This painted terra-cotta plaque, with traces of polychrome decoration, features the iconography of Xipe-Totec, "The Flayed One," an ancient Mixtec deity adopted by the Aztecs. God of vegetation and protector of goldsmiths, he was represented as covered with a flayed human skin.

WESTERN MEXICO

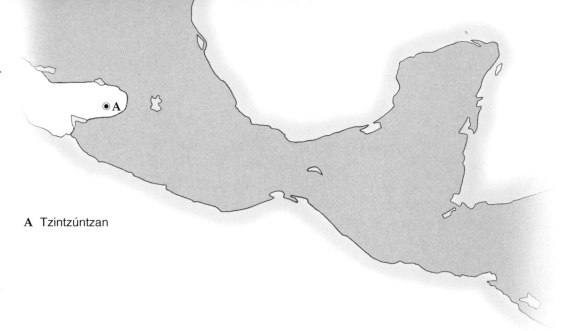

A Tzintzúntzan

While the artistic output of Guerrero reveals a certain receptiveness to other cultures, such as that of the Olmecs of the Preclassic Period and later that of Teotihuacan, the outlying regions remained isolated artistically.

The pottery forms may not be particularly sophisticated, but they are of great interest as they generally depict scenes from the daily lives and customs of the people who made them. They include representations of animals, dancers, fools, shamans, acrobats, and warriors. There are also images that relate to the ritual ball game, although this was not played in precisely the same way as in the other cultural centers. Remains found in the tombs have provided evidence of the cult of trophy heads and human sacrifices.

During the Post-Classic Period, one of the peoples of Michoacán, the Tarascan, began to dominate the others. Their capital, with pyramidal temples, was at Tzintzúntzan and they were long a thorn in the side of the Aztecs. A Tarascan speciality was the working of gold and copper using techniques passed along trade routes from Peru and Colombia. They were the only Mesoamerican people to use metal weapons and "money" in the form of copper axes.

To complete this overview of Pre-Columbian Mexico and the various populations that inhabited it, we must now mention the cultures that developed on the margins of the great civilizations, particularly in the extreme west of Mexico. These territories include the present-day states of Guerrero, Colima, Michoacan, Jalisco, Nayarit, and Sinaloa. In these regions small kingdoms were formed, of modest extent and ruled by a nobleman known as "cacique."

During the Classic Period, the population was probably concentrated in rural villages; no monumental works have been discovered and most of our evidence consists of finds from tombs, especially abundant ceramics.

74 (left) The cultures that developed in the regions of western Mexico produced relatively simple, popular art forms lacking the magnificence and complex iconography of the other Mesoamerican civilizations. This attractive Chupícuaro figurine portrays a two-headed female deity.

74 (right) Nayarit pottery often depicts couples and lively groups in natural poses from everyday life with directness and charm. Here a couple is depicted seated close together, the woman holding a vessel in her hand. Both wear a headdress and nose rings. Details of their clothes are represented with painted geometric motifs.

75 (below) This attractive painted terra-cotta statuette is a Chupícuaro piece, probably representing a female figure. The brightly patterned painted geometric motifs may reproduce textiles.

75 (right) A typical example of Nayarit artistic production, this female figure is in a seated position with her legs crossed and holding a pointed object in her hand, perhaps a sacrificial knife or a tool.

76 (below) Rather than remains of large ceremonial centers, the civilizations of western Mexico have left tombs containing fascinating funerary assemblages rich in terra-cotta figures, like the one shown here.

Made by the Colima people it again depicts a human figure, realized with great simplicity and realism. Perhaps it is a dignitary, a priest, or a ball game player.

76 (above) This vessel in the shape of a dog is also a product of the Colima culture of western Mexico. Numerous terra-cotta dogs have been found in the shaft-tombs, along with skeletons of dogs sacrificed to accompany the dead. In the Mesoamerican world dogs were commonly raised as food.

77 (left) This seated male figure dressed in a fantastic costume was perhaps a jester. The Colima people, like others of western Mexico, have left a rich iconography relating to jesters and jugglers who provided entertainment at popular festivities.

77 (below left) In addition to human figures, Colima pottery also depicts many different kinds of animals. This brick-red, highly polished vessel representing a parrot dates to AD 100.

77 (above) At the court of the Aztec ruler Motecuhzoma II, the Spaniards noted the presence of many dwarfs and hunchbacks, who were treated with great deference, almost as if they were divine.

A similar custom was undoubtedly practiced by the peoples of western Mexico, as shown by this graceful vessel depicting a hunchbacked figure with his feet placed on strange supports and leaning on a stick.

THE CONQUEST AND THE END OF A WORLD

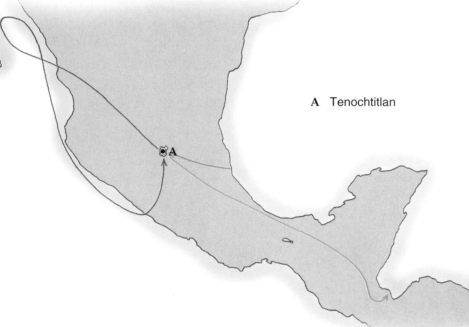

→ 1519   The expeditions
→ 1524–1526   of Hernán Cortés
→ 1535

A   Tenochtitlan

78 (center left) This illustration from the Historia de las Indias, written in 1579 by the Spanish chronicler Diego de Durán, depicts the appearance of a comet above Motecuhzoma II. This was just one of many strange portents that foretold terrible events, including the end of his reign.

78–79 (below) A page from the Historia de las Indias depicting a battle between the Conquistadores and the Aztecs. On the left can be seen the Spanish army, led by Pedro de Alvarado, a companion of Hernán Cortés; on the right is the Aztec army represented by soldiers belonging to the military orders of the Eagle and the Jaguar. The Spanish armies, taking advantage of Motecuhzoma II's diplomacy and hospitality, defeated the last empire of Pre-Columbian Mesoamerica in a series of bloody and terrible battles, won with their superior weapons.

78 (left) Also taken from the account of Diego de Durán, an important historical document about the era of the Spanish Conquest, this illustration depicts a meeting between the Spanish captain Hernán Cortés and a native woman, La Malinche, who became his interpreter and mistress.

In 1519, following a series of dire omens in the form of strange astronomical phenomena, Motecuhzoma II was informed of the arrival in his land of bearded, light-skinned foreigners: the Spanish Conquistadores led by Hernán Cortés. As was to be the case fourteen years later with Atahualpa, the Inca ruler of Peru, Motecuhzoma was convinced that he was witnessing the enactment of an ancient prophecy handed down by his ancestors, in this case one that spoke of the return of Quetzalcoatl, the Feathered Serpent.

The European invaders were received at Tenochtitlan with great honor. They described the city, with its magnificent palaces and gardens on floating islands, as a "second Venice." The soldiers were considered as divine messengers and were presented with gifts and tributes. As soon as they realized what was happening the Spaniards astutely and cynically took advantage of Motecuhzoma and, in a series of bloody battles, crushed the last empire of Pre-Columbian Mesoamerica.

The Aztec civilization along with its written records, material culture, and traditions, was mercilessly eradicated within just a few years. Of the 20 to 25 million inhabitants of Mexico at that time, only one in ten survived. The population was wiped out by war and disease. Motecuhzoma's successor died of smallpox, and the last ruler of Tenochtitlan, Cuauhtemóc, after heroically resisting the invaders, eventually surrendered in 1521. Cortés's triumph placed the entire country under the rule of the Spanish crown and led to the creation of the colony known as New Spain.

79 (top) When Motecuhzoma II heard of the arrival by sea of the "white and bearded men" he dispatched messengers laden with gifts to meet them, interpreting the event as the promised return of the mythical god-hero Quetzalcoatl. This image, taken from the account by Diego de Durán, shows a native messenger offering a necklace to Cortés.

79 (right) This bloody image records a scene from the battle of Tenochtitlan, during which the Aztec army was wiped out by the Conquistadores. The history of the Mexica people concluded with the treacherous killing of the emperor and the total destruction of the capital Tenochtitlan, the territory of which was annexed to Spain in 1521.

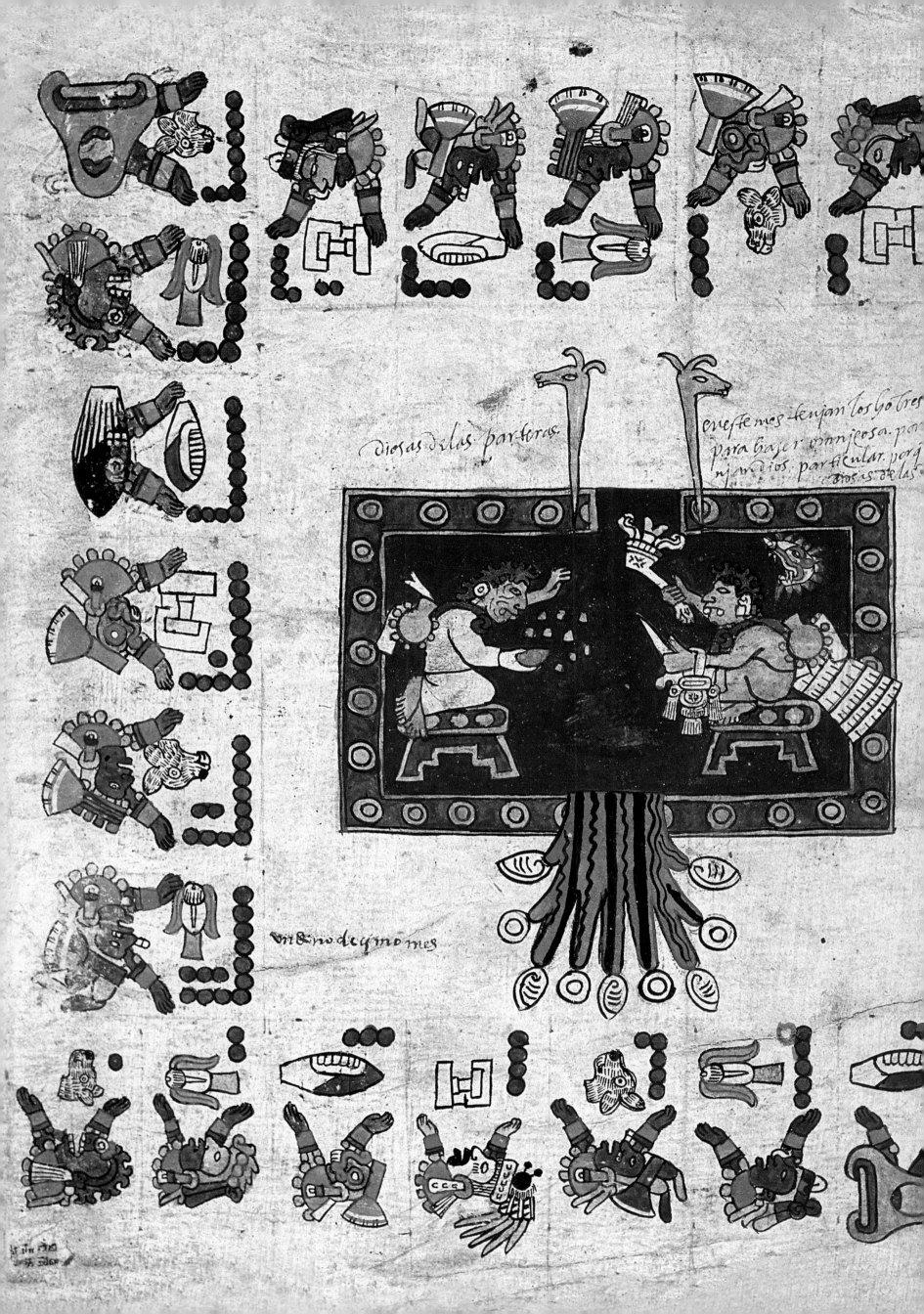

diosas delas parteras.

eneste mes tenjan los ho[m]bres
para baze[r] vina[...]osa. po[...]
n[...]on dios. particular. por[...]
diosas delas

vn&no de gmomes

DAILY LIFE, ART, AND RELIGION OF THE PEOPLES OF MESOAMERICA

80–81 The myths, history, and details of the everyday life of the Aztecs have come down to us in the pages of the painted codices. Plate 21 from the Codex Borbonicus, reproduced here, depicts a scene of the creator god and goddess, surrounded by calendrical glyphs.

81 (left) This somewhat picturesque depiction of the god Quetzalcoatl, one of the pre-eminent figures in the complex pantheon of Mesoamerica, is taken from Historia de las Indias *by Diego de Durán.*

THE SOURCES

Our knowledge of the historical events and culture of many Pre-Columbian civilizations is derived in part from archaeology: the temples and palaces excavated in ceremonial centers, the sculptures, ceramics, and funerary treasures from the tombs. Of the various forms of writing used by Pre-Columbian peoples, only those of the Maya and the Aztecs have been deciphered so far, and even they have yet to reveal all their secrets.

By the early 16th century, when the first contacts between the European

Around the same time in the Yucatán, the Europeans came into contact with the survivors of the Post-Classic Maya civilization. After years of bloody rebellions the natives were subjected to the supremacy of the Spanish only in 1546.

The Maya and the Aztecs, and to a lesser extent the Mixtecs and the Olmecs, have handed down to the present day at least part of their history, not only through the archaeological remains of their material culture, but also through

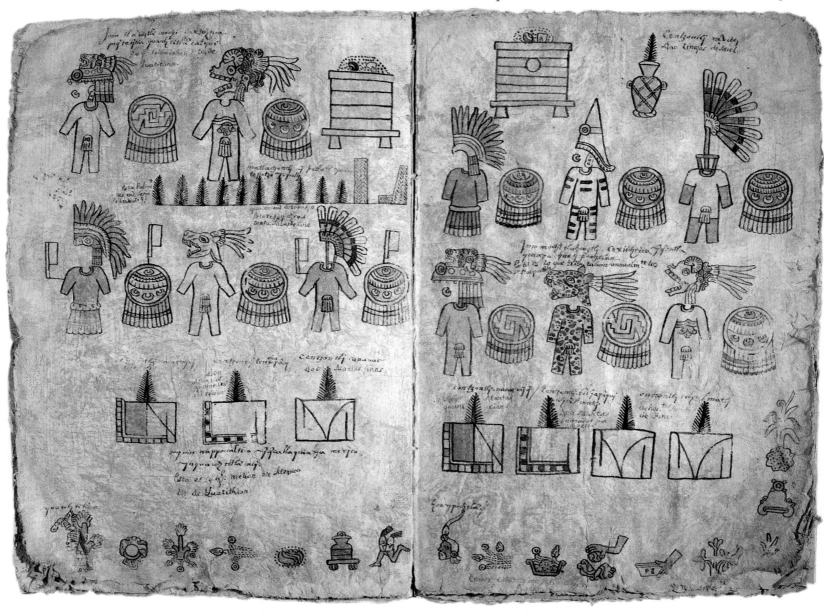

82 (above) The Aztecs are the Mesoamerican people we know most about, thanks to the fascinating painted illustrations in their codices. This page from the Codex Mendoza depicts the items required as tribute to the ruler of Tenochtitlan, including furniture, clothes, warrior costumes, weapons, and boxes of food.

83 (opposite) The Codex Borbonicus is a text of 36 pages, containing illustrations of the Aztec Ritual Calendar of 260 days and the festivals and rituals linked to it. The symbolism is complex. A page depicting a ceremony linked with fertility and the cult of Tlaloc is shown here.

invaders and the Mesoamerican world took place, many of the ancient civilizations had long since declined or had been absorbed and dominated by the Aztecs. It was therefore only with the Aztecs, at the height of their cultural development and territorial expansion, that the Spanish came into direct contact. We have their own accounts of their astonishment at the magnificence of Tenochtitlan and the court of Motecuhzoma II, and the daily lives of the ordinary people.

written documents from the pre-Colonial era and records gathered by the missionaries during the centuries following the Conquest.

These records, despite all their omissions and inadequacies, have shed light on many aspects of the history, thought, and daily life of these civilizations. Through the traditions handed down by the Maya and Aztecs, information about other Mesoamerican peoples has also been gleaned: fragments of history mixed

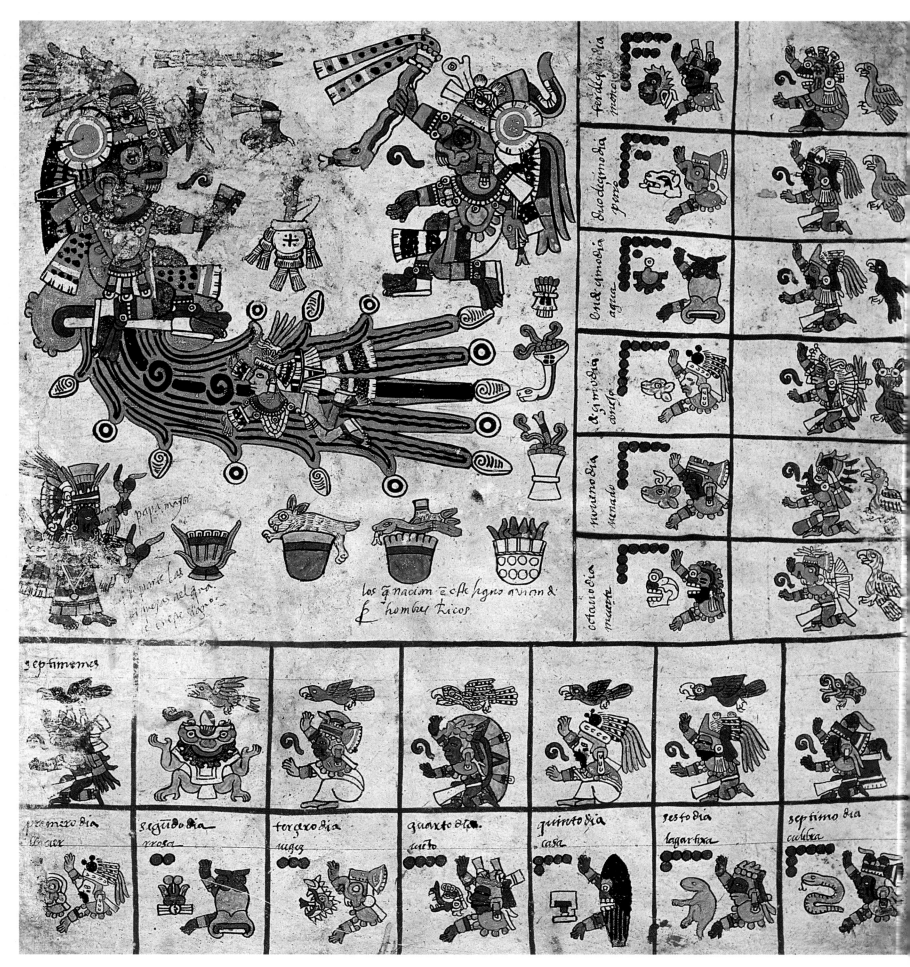

with legend that can in part be married with archaeological evidence.

Written sources relating to the Maya are rarer and take the form of four books from the pre-Colonial era, known as "codices," and a number of ancient religious texts transcribed in the Roman alphabet by literate natives after the Conquest. These include the Popol Vuh and the Books of Chilám Balám.

There are also the testimonies of a number of Spanish priests, among which the most comprehensive and informative is *La Relación de las Cosas de Yucatán*, written by the Spanish bishop Diego de Landa in the second half of the 16th century. After having "eradicated" the cults of the Maya and forcefully converting the people to Catholicism, Landa burned all the idols and ancient books kept in the temples, destroying forever a heritage of inestimable value. Perhaps, after having committed this act, the bishop realized that the culture and people of Yucatán actually had many aspects of great interest. He therefore proceeded to compile a work which represents a faithful and detailed description of the lives of the surviving groups of Maya he encountered.

When reading Landa's accounts we must not forget that some of his interpretations were based on his Christian and European point of view. Nonetheless, thanks to his account we have received a body of information regarding the daily life, festivals,

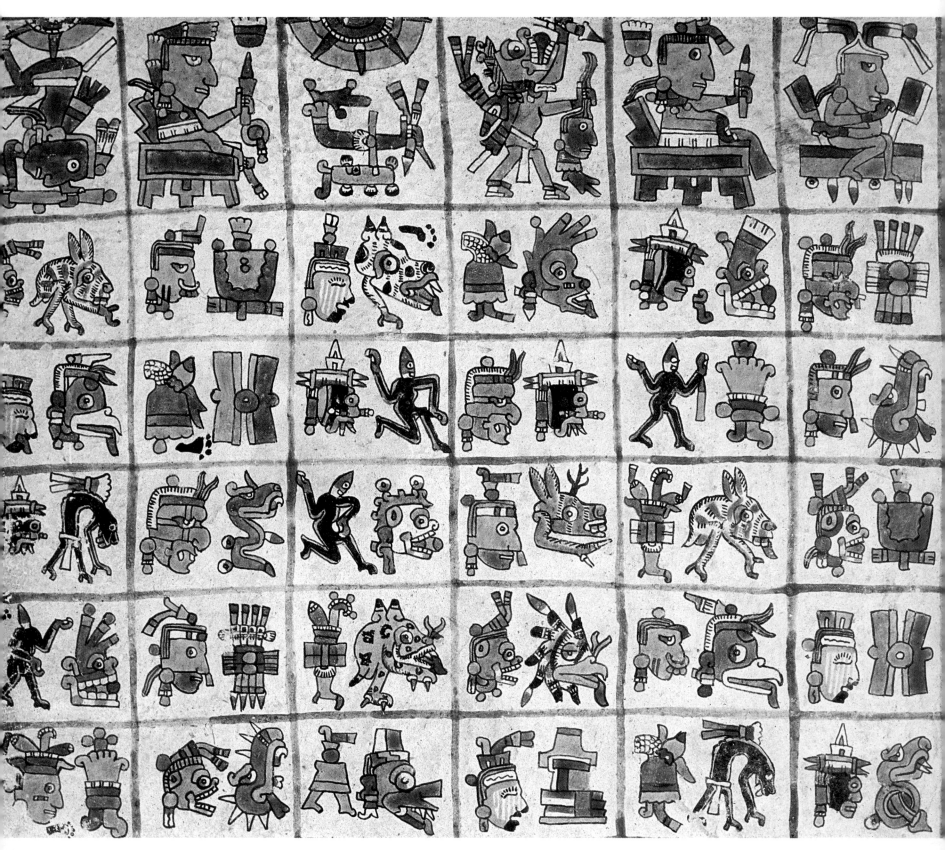

dress, calendar, and ancestral religious practices that were still current in the 16th century. It should be emphasized that this information relates only to the final period of the Maya civilization, the last centuries of the Post-Classic, which had long been open to Toltec cultural influences. Virtually nothing is known, in contrast, about the daily life of the ordinary people of the Classic Period. Inscriptions in stone that are still being deciphered narrate the history of the ruling dynasties, while vase paintings illustrate scenes of court life.

More Aztec codices have survived, some written before the Conquest while others were transcribed onto European paper by literate native scribes once the Spaniards had begun to show an interest in the culture of the conquered peoples. The codices, which use a form of pictographic writing, illustrate with a wealth of detail the history of the Aztec people, complete with relative dates, and also aspects of daily life, religious practices, and festivals linked to various cults and the calendar.

There are also numerous texts written by Spanish monks or by natives converted to Catholicism. Among the former are Bernardino de Sahagún and Diego de Durán, as well as many others. These authors amassed a vast range of written records relating to the customs of the Aztec people, some of which they had witnessed themselves, while for others they drew on older sources or the accounts of the natives. Although, as with the work of Landa, these texts are filtered through a Christian and European point of view, they constitute an extremely rich and interesting source of information on the lives and customs current in the reign of Motecuhzoma II.

Before we embark on an examination of the most interesting aspects of the society and daily life of both the Maya of the Post-Classic period and the Aztecs in particular— a world very distant in terms of time

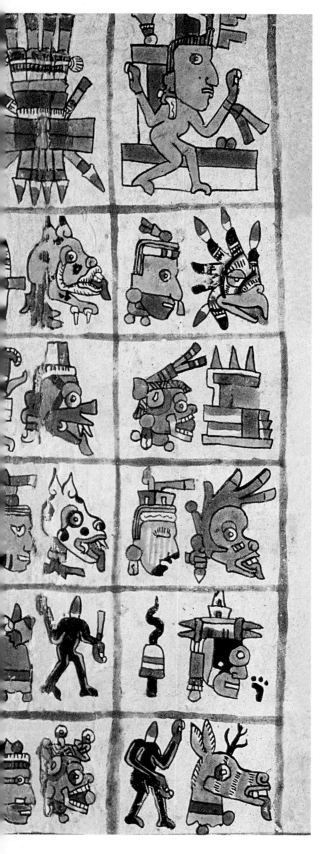

84–85 (left) The Codex Cospi, also known as the Codex Bolognese, from the city where it is conserved, is a pictographic divinatory text, made of five deer skins glued together to form a long strip. It deals above all with the Ritual Calendar of 260 days, known as tonalpohualli, the symbols of which appear in the page shown here.

85 (center) This illustration is taken from the Codex Borbonicus, one of the richest and most interesting of the Aztec manuscripts. Here, four priests are feeding the flames during the New Fire ceremony at Tenochtitlan. A comparable ritual was also practiced by the Maya, as described by Diego de Landa.

85 (bottom) The Codex Borbonicus is a screenfold book of bark paper. Most of its pages are painted with the tonalpohualli, or ritual calendar. In the center of this scene depicting a religious ceremony is a maize and earth deity.

and milieu—it is vital that we understand that in Pre-Columbian America even the most ordinary events had a profound religious significance. The birth of a child, a bolt of lightning, or the growth of the maize crop were seen not as simple occurrences, but were read as manifestations of divine will. War, dance, and the study of the stars and their movements were all means of communicating with the supernatural world. By looking at numerous aspects and recognizing a concept of the world far removed from our own, we can begin to establish intellectual contact with the fragments of the ancient Pre-Columbian civilizations.

THE FAMILY, EDUCATION, FOOD, AND THE HOME

Mayan inscriptions of the Classic Period provide precise information about members of the royal families who lived in the courts of the city states. In certain cases, for example at Palenque, female figures emerge as queens who had dominant roles in the dynastic sequence, and analysis has shown that in some circumstances succession to the throne passed through the maternal line.

Among the nobility, polygamy was fairly common and we find the names of kings associated with those of different wives. However, it appears that this custom was not so frequent

86 (center) A mother and midwife are about to bathe a new-born baby, in this drawing from Bernardino de Sahagún's Historia *de las Cosas de Nueva España. The birth of a child was a very important occasion, accompanied by ritual cleansing.*

among the lower classes. Weddings represented an occasion for great ceremony even for the poorest families, and were accompanied by elaborate celebrations and rituals. For the man, among the fundamental criteria in his choice of a future wife were star signs: any incompatibility of the astral conjunctions at the moment of the couple's births represented an insurmountable obstacle to the marriage. Once the "astrological" harmony had been established, a person was chosen to negotiate the dowry the young woman was required to bring to her future parents-in-law. This generally consisted of valued objects such as feathers, cacao, precious stones, and cotton cloth. The wedding ceremony was not necessarily conducted by a member of the priesthood: if the parents were not sufficiently wealthy the priest would be replaced by a village elder or a local governor.

The officiant proceeded by knotting together the hems of the cloaks worn by the couple, blessing them and exhorting them to act wisely. After the ceremony there was a banquet with music and dancing. Bartolomeo de Las Casas recorded a particularly unusual fact about the wedding night:

two old women had the task of accompanying the young couple to their home and staying with them throughout the night to instruct them about their future sex life.

More precise information is available about the Aztecs' complex pre-marital rituals. The wedding could be held when the young man was twenty years of age and the woman sixteen. In the case of the more well-to-do classes, the parents were not the only figures who had the right to approve or disapprove of a proposed marriage, this right was also held by the educators in the schools.

As in the Maya world, no marriage could go ahead unless there was at least some astrological compatibility between the couple. Once the religious rituals and the sumptuous banquets that followed the wedding ceremony had been completed the marriage could be consummated. Subsequently, the young husband would receive a portion of land from the *calpolli*, the "clan" to which he belonged. He could retain part of the agricultural produce for himself and his family and in this way the couple was inserted into the social structure of the community. To the Aztecs adultery was something akin to

homicide: if anyone other than the partner witnessed the act, the guilty parties would immediately be tortured and condemned to death by stoning.

In both Maya and Aztec cultures the family was the fundamental social unit. The contemporary chroniclers recorded a series of interesting facts regarding pregnancy and birth in both societies. When a woman went into labor she was assisted by one or more midwives, who were also in charge of magical and religious rituals. These midwives had the task of alleviating the suffering of the future mother with special potions with sedative properties made from herbs and by placing a previously purified warm stone on her abdomen. Rituals were performed in honor of the deities of birth and female fertility, Ixchel for the Maya and Tlarolteotl for the Aztecs, to ensure health and divine protection for the baby. There was also a purification ritual for the new-born baby involving water, similar to the Christian practice of baptism.

Archaeology has confirmed that many peoples of Pre-Columbian America practiced cranial deformation of very young children. Diego de Landa provides an interesting account of this practice among the Maya: he explains that a few days after the birth, the baby was laid on its back and its still soft head was gripped between two wooden panels, one placed on the back of the head and other on the forehead. This practice flattened the cranium in accordance with the aesthetic preferences of the era.

Aztec children were educated by their parents until adolescence. From the age of fifteen young males continued their education at a sort of military academy known as telpochcalli, a Nahuatl word meaning

"House of Youths." From the time of Motecuhzoma I, education had been made compulsory for all boys, whatever their social class. Each calpolli had its own telpochcalli that operated on a college basis, where the boys received a dual form of teaching, with the aim of transforming them into exemplary citizens and subjects, and also to train them in the art of war. The teachers taught their pupils to respect and serve the elderly, the nobility, and the sovereign. Aztec education included the study of music, singing, and dance, fundamental elements of all festivities. This lighter side of the programme, however, provided no exemption from the study of the techniques of warfare, military discipline, and the use of weapons.

A second type of school was the calmecac, a kind of seminary that was reserved on the whole for the children of the upper class. In general calmecacs were attached to a temple and were run by members of the priesthood. The education they imparted was far more complex than that provided by the public schools. Pupils were again admitted at the age of fifteen and were taught writing, calendric computation, astronomy, and divination. These were all disciplines reserved for a privileged few. Young men who wished to could forego marriage and continue to study and subsequently take up a religious career. The schools were also open to the daughters of the nobility, though they were strictly segregated from the boys. They were educated by female teachers in dance, music, cooking, and weaving. Their period of strict training was completed only when they reached a marriageable age.

Information about Maya education is sparser, but it is presumed that it was a privilege of the well-to-do.

Diego de Landa mentioned the extreme respect girls were obliged to show to their mothers. The latter were expected to educate their daughters, teach them a trade, and to punish them severely if disobedient.

Agriculture was the principal source of food for the Mesoamerican peoples, supplemented by hunting and fishing. The most widely cultivated plant and the staple source of food was maize, a crop unknown in Europe until the discovery of America. The Maya and the Aztecs, as well as other groups, made offerings and sacrifices to the god of maize: the spilling of blood was thought necessary to feed the earth and to ensure abundant harvests. Maize was eaten either boiled or roasted, while maize flour was used in the preparation of a number of staple dishes such as tortillas and tamales. Other common crops included tomatoes (tomatl in Nahuatl), many species of beans, pumpkins, chilli peppers, pineapples, and avocados. Most of these were not seen in Europe until after the 16th century.

From the earliest times the most highly prized crop apart from maize was cacao. The celebrations devoted to the god of the cacao plant and the

privileges enjoyed by cacao growers in Maya society are evidence of the importance of this plant. A powder was obtained by grinding the beans, which was mixed with water to obtain an exquisite drink known to the Aztecs as *xocolatl*. They, like the Maya and other groups, drank it cold, bitter, and flavored with various substances including vanilla or chilli. In tombs of the Maya nobility of the Classic Period and those of Mixtec aristocracy, archaeologists have found painted vessels of various shapes that were used to contain the chocolate drink.

Other plants cultivated included cotton, which was woven, as were the fibers obtained from the leaves of the agave. In contrast with the abundance of fruit and vegetables, the ancient Mesoamericans had little livestock: among the species domesticated were the turkey and the dog, an animal considered perfectly edible. Abundant game provided most of the meat consumed, and the lakes were rich in fish and shellfish. Another widespread agricultural activity was apiculture, or beekeeping. Honey was used in the preparation of various foods and for sweetening alcoholic drinks and other beverages; in fact both sugar beet and cane were unknown in Pre-Columbian America.

Excavations at Maya cities of the Classic Period have revealed the presence of numerous stone buildings, generally grouped around large courtyards, that were probably the residences of dignitaries or members of the nobility. In contrast there are few traces of the houses of ordinary people, which were located outside the urban area and would have been built of perishable materials. A number of images from the Post-Classic Period, however, illustrate examples of Yucatán domestic architecture of the period. The best known are reliefs depicting a stylized house used as a decorative element on the sides of the arch at Labná. A fresco at Chichén Itzá shows an example of a circular hut, probably constructed in a local regional style.

We have better information about the homes at Tenochtitlan. On the outskirts of the capital the fishermen lived in huts built of canes and straw, while within the city the homes varied from modest stone-built houses to noble palaces. The homes of the middle class were built of adobe, sun-dried mud bricks, or of stone and adobe. As the city was founded on a lake, the buildings were constructed on a platform of stone to provide insulation from ground water.

Aztec houses were rectangular in plan and the walls were usually finished in white or bright colors. The rooms, the number of which varied according to the social standing of the family, faced onto a large patio, a central courtyard where rainwater was collected, dogs and turkeys roamed, and flowers were grown. Inside the house there were usually one or more bedrooms for the whole family, a small shrine, a bathroom, and a kitchen in which the hearth was located. More modest buildings

consisted of a single multi-function room, with the hearth situated in the courtyard, protected by a canopy. The most carefully tended part of the house was the small shrine where the ancestral gods were venerated. The steam room is a typical Aztec feature, though the Maya also had saunas or steam rooms. The constant cleansing of the body and the hair was not simply a matter of hygiene, but had strong associations with ritual purification. The most widely used method of purification was the *temazcalli*, a steam bath found in the homes of the middle class, noble residences, and in public baths.

The houses contained very little furniture: there were no tables, chairs, or beds. People slept on a mat, known as a *petatl*, wrapped in cotton covers. Apart from the hearth that served both for cooking food and heating the house in the cooler months, the kitchen contained all kinds of vessels, utensils, a loom, and the *metate*, a low table of volcanic rock on which maize was ground with a pestle.

There were no windows in the houses: light and air entered through the doorway covered with a straw mat. Roofs were not tiled but were composed of a structure of wooden poles covered with a layer of thatch. Many houses were built along canals and almost all the inhabitants would have owned a canoe which they would moor close to the entrance. Structurally, the palaces of the nobles were not very different from more modest houses, but were larger and had more sophisticated furnishings.

DRESS

Pottery decorations, wall paintings, reliefs, and terra-cotta statuettes provide detailed information about the clothing worn by the elite of the Mayan courts of the Classic Period—not only the resplendent ceremonial costumes, but also those worn in battle.

Analysis of these images clearly shows that clothing was only one element—and not the most important—of the ornamentation of the person. Kings and nobles wore a simple loincloth made of a band of white cotton wound between the legs and around the waist, usually decorated with pearls and colored feathers. The shoulders were covered

90 (above) In the Classic Period the Maya of the island of Jaina produced sophisticated and original pottery forms, in particular a type of anthropomorphic clay figurine. These frequently depicted high-ranking figures, nobles, and shamans, but also more humble people such as the celebrated "weaver." This example represents a woman whose attributes—scepter and fan—undoubtedly place her in an elevated caste.

90 (right) These elegant examples of Maya jewelry are a pair of shell disks for the ears. They are engraved with the profile of a man.

with a cloak elegantly embroidered or covered with feathers. In certain images, such as the wall paintings at Bonampak, this cotton garment is replaced by a jaguar skin, worn only in ceremonial contexts. However, what distinguished high-ranking Maya from the rest of the population were their headdresses, hairstyles and jewelry.

Sophisticated terra-cotta figurines produced on the island of Jaina provide numerous examples of magnificent headdresses—conical, spiral, or crowned with plumes. It is presumed that these headdresses were supported with a rigid structure of wood or reed. Feathers had a value

91 (above) An idea of the clothes and jewelry worn by women in Pre-Columbian Mesoamerica is provided by this delightful Totonac clay figurine dating from around AD 500.

91 (right) This Maya figure has a solemn, majestic air that suggests that the subject belonged to the priesthood. The conical headdress, feathered cloak, and a kind of loincloth are clearly shown. The crossed legs, raised arm, and contemplative look of the figure suggest meditation.

90 (opposite, below right) The details of this Jaina-style clay figurine provide a wonderful picture of the richness of the clothing and jewelry worn by the Maya nobility of the Classic Period. The ear discs and the elaborate headdress that still retains traces of blue paint are particularly spectacular.

91 (above) Elegance and great dignity characterize this clay figurine, another example of the Jaina style dating from the Classic Period. The figure is shown in a seated position with legs crossed. The large necklace and mutilation of the mouth indicate that the subject belonged to a high social class.

similar to that of jewels: the greatest royal symbol was the plume of emerald green feathers of the quetzál, a tropical bird held sacred and much prized throughout Mesoamerica, but which today is almost extinct.

Nobles of both sexes adorned themselves with rings, anklets, ear spools, bracelets, necklaces, and breastplates in jadeite, serpentine, bone, and mother-of-pearl. Gold and silver were unknown until the Post-Classic Period when it appeared at Chichén Itzá, through contacts with lower Central America.

Rare female images from the Classic Period probably depict priestesses and queens. These figures are shown wearing cloaks and headdresses richly decorated like those of the males. One example is the relief decorating Lintel 24 at Yaxchilán in which the exquisite dress of Lady Xoc, the wife of Shield Jaguar, is depicted with a wealth of detail.

Landa's descriptions of the Maya-Yucatec costumes of the 16th century illustrate a type of simple female dress worn by the women of the coastal villages: a long cotton skirt and a knotted cloak that covered the shoulders and breasts. Inland, however, women wore a long, waisted cotton tunic, open on two sides, that has evolved into the traditional dress of contemporary Maya women known as a *huipil*.

92 (below left) Durán's manuscript Historia de las Indias, *provides detailed illustrations of the costumes and clothing worn by the Aztec nobility. This drawing shows a man wearing a cotton loincloth and a colored cloak, holding a sumptuous fan of feathers.*

92–93 (above) Among the peoples of Mesoamerica headdresses and jewelry were more highly regarded than clothing and represented symbols of power. This superb feather headdress was perhaps presented by Motecuhzoma II to Cortés, who then sent it to the emperor Charles V.

92 (left) The Maya and the Aztecs excelled in the skill of featherwork. This fan consists of feathers of many different colors which have been cut and glued to a wooden support creating a stylized butterfly motif in the center.

According to the historical sources and the painted illustrations of the codices, Aztec dress was not greatly different from that of the Maya. For the men, the two principal garments were the *maxtlatl*, an embroidered cotton loincloth, and the *tilmatli*, a rectangular piece of cotton that was knotted over the left shoulder. When seated this cloak was spread in front of the knees so as to cover the entire body. The *tilmatli* was usually white and was decorated with colored borders with geometric or animal motifs. Leading members of the elite occasionally wore cloaks dyed turquoise or covered with feathers and rabbit fur. Certain sources, in particular the Codex Magliabechiano and the Florentine Codex of Sahagún, reproduce with great precision the vivid colors of the

93 (top) The Mixtecs, were highly skilled in working gold. They frequently combined it with precious stones, such as turquoise, to create splendid jewels, as this pendant illustrates.

93 (center) Spectacular items of jewelry in gold and precious stones, such as this necklace of gold and turquoise, have been found in the tombs of Monte Albán. Knowledge of the techniques of working gold spread from Ecuador.

93 (bottom) An extremely elegant Mixtec breastplate made of gold, coral, and turquoise. In the Mesoamerican world both men and women wore jewelry, which was an important part of their dress.

clothing worn by members of the aristocracy and the priesthood at Tenochtitlan. The men of the lower social classes wore a coarser *tilmatli* woven from agave fiber. Aztec women usually wore long cotton tunics belted at the waist with a band of fabric with decorated borders known as a *cueitl*, and a triangular cotton blouse, the equivalent of the *huipil* still worn by the Maya today.

The most highly prized fabrics came from the Veracruz region where the Huaxtec weavers decorated their white cotton garments with brightly colored animal motifs.

For the feet the most common form of footwear was the *cactli*, a kind of sandal with a sole of plant fiber or animal skin laced to the ankle with cords.

In both the Aztec and Maya cultural contexts, the various jewels and ornaments in precious stones, mother-of-pearl, and quetzál feathers, together with the headdresses, hairstyles, and tattoos, always reflected the social standing of those who wore them and had precise symbolic connotations.

In contrast with earlier civilizations, the Aztecs also had gold and silver ornaments produced by highly skilled Mixtec and Tarascan craftsmen.

94 (below) Mixtec mastery of the goldsmith's art reached extremely high levels, as indicated by items in funerary assemblages from the tombs of Monte Albán, such as this elegant bracelet.

94 (bottom) The Mixtec gold necklace and bracelet shown here are made of numerous elements in the shape of a turtle-shell from which hang tiny rattles.

94–95 (below, center) When the Aztec rulers came into contact with the goldsmith's art of the Mixtec peoples, they imported the artists to their courts in order to be able to adorn themselves with all kinds of gold jewelry. Many Aztec nobles commissioned the goldsmiths to create elaborate and extravagant necklaces, often hung with tiny bells, indicating their high rank.

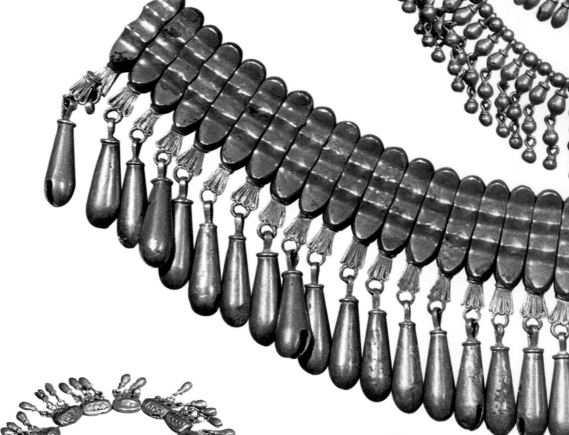

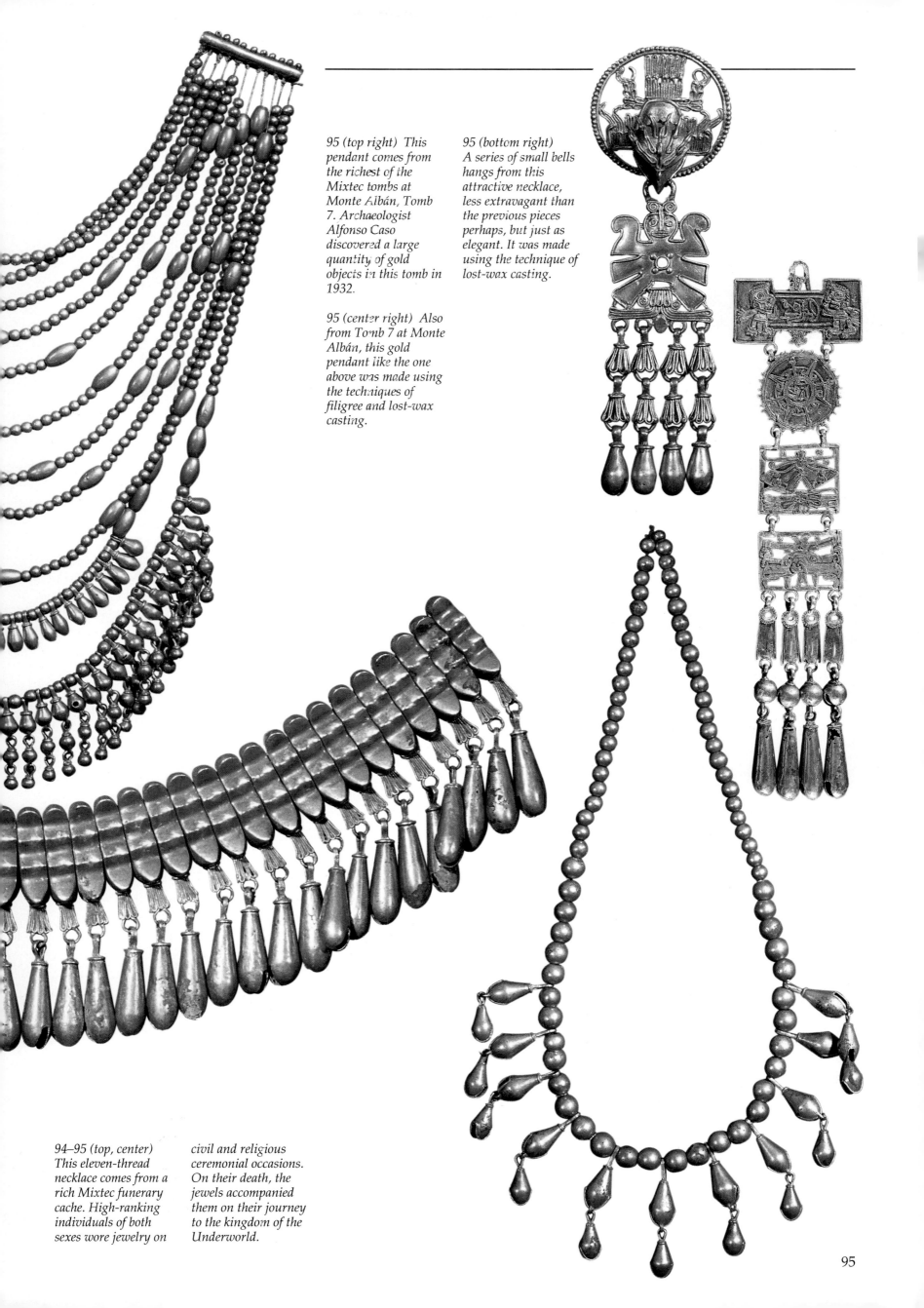

95 (top right) This pendant comes from the richest of the Mixtec tombs at Monte Albán, Tomb 7. Archaeologist Alfonso Caso discovered a large quantity of gold objects in this tomb in 1932.

95 (center right) Also from Tomb 7 at Monte Albán, this gold pendant like the one above was made using the techniques of filigree and lost-wax casting.

95 (bottom right) A series of small bells hangs from this attractive necklace, less extravagant than the previous pieces perhaps, but just as elegant. It was made using the technique of lost-wax casting.

94–95 (top, center) This eleven-thread necklace comes from a rich Mixtec funerary cache. High-ranking individuals of both sexes wore jewelry on civil and religious ceremonial occasions. On their death, the jewels accompanied them on their journey to the kingdom of the Underworld.

MUSIC AND DANCE

As in all ancient civilizations, music and dance played an important role in the daily lives of the peoples of Mesoamerica. Archaeological and historical sources testify to the variety of musical instruments and types of dance in the different regions. In the case of the Maya and Aztec civilizations, as probably with other peoples, music, singing, and dancing accompanied religious ceremonies, marriages, funerals, sacrifices, and coronations, as well as the festivities linked to the calendric cycles.

Evidence also survives from other cultures: many terra-cotta vessels from western Mexico depict musicians and scenes of individual or collective dances, often associated with the ritual of self-sacrifice. Numerous figurines from central

96 (left) Absorbed in the dance, this naked male Mayan terra-cotta figurine holds flowers and is wearing a coyote mask on his head.

96 (top) A trio of Aztec musicians composed of a singer and two men playing pipes provide music for a festival. This illustration is from a colonial-era manuscript.

96 (center) In this illustration from a 16th-century manuscript a "band" of Aztec musicians accompanies the dancers. The musicians are playing on percussion instruments, probably drums made of wood and deer skin, while the dancers are holding fans and flowers.

Veracruz, with their hands raised almost as if in prayer, portray a sacred dance. The Mixtec Codex Selden contains painted images illustrating a complicated marriage dance. Recent research by epigraphists has shed new light on a number of sacred dances of the Maya courts of the Classic Period. One of these involved a trance-like dance with boa constrictors.

Dances also accompanied many self-sacrifice rituals: the nobles and the king, under the effect of psychotropic drugs, perforated their genitals with a pair of wooden sticks covered with colored cloth known as "the wings of the dancers." Once they had entered a hallucinatory state the protagonists began a careful dance during which they offered their blood. Another type of dance was dedicated to the Maize God: in this case the dignitaries were

flanked by a group servants—dwarfs and hunchbacks—who imitated the waving of the leaves of maize plants in the wind with movements of their arms and hands. Many Maya vase paintings from the Classic Period illustrate scenes of macabre dances set in the Xibalbá, the Kingdom of the Dead or Underworld, that feature skeletons, mythical beings, and animals. These scenes are reminiscent of descriptions of the "Place of Fright" contained in the sacred text known as the Popol Vuh.

Sources from the Colonial period describe spectacular dances and parades that were

97 (above) A dancer makes graceful movements in honor of the Maize God, as indicated by the symbol of the cob, in this attractive Mayan terra-cotta whistle of the late Classic Period.

97 (right) Whistles were common to all Mesoamerican peoples, along with other wind and percussion instruments, whereas string instruments were unknown. This whistle in polychrome terra-cotta is a Mayan piece and depicts a maracas player.

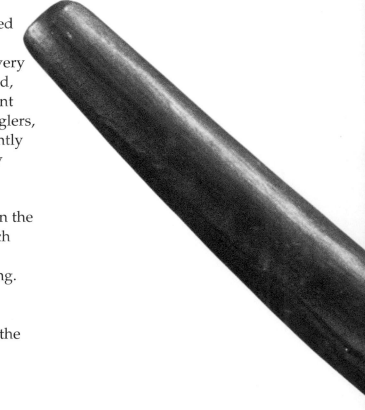

still held in the streets of the cities and villages in honor of the ancient deities and during the festivals linked to the various months of the year. These accounts are of great interest, revealing the coexistence of ancestral cultural elements with more recent influences foreign to the Yucatán area.

Bernardino de Sahagún provides numerous accounts of Aztec dances and festivals, in particular ones held to celebrate the individual months. Certain dances were reserved for men, others for women, while yet others were open to both sexes. Generally, the parades took place at the foot of the temple dedicated to the divinity being honored in the ceremony. In many cases the dancers wore masks,

a tradition that probably originated in Olmec times or before.

One type of spectacle that was very common in the Post-Classic period, but almost certainly of very ancient origins, was that provided by jugglers, acrobats, and clowns who frequently were dwarfs or hunchbacks. They would perform frenzied dances, comedies, and farces for the enjoyment of the courts but also in the streets of the poorest villages. Such shows and dances were always accompanied by music and singing.

The oldest image relating to a musician was found in western Mexico. The painted codices and the archaeological remains provide detailed evidence of the range of

98 (opposite above)
Maya and Aztec
musical instruments
played during
religious and civic
festivities and
ceremonies were often
true works of art,
beautifully designed
and rich in decoration.
This is a teponaztli,
a horizontal wooden
drum used by the
Aztecs. The drum was
beaten with balls of
natural rubber and
produced two different
tones. This example
dates to the 16th
century.

98 (opposite below)
The surface of this
beautiful teponaztli,
made from a hollow
trunk, has been carved
in the form of an owl.

99 (top) An Aztec
instrument, this terra-
cotta ocarina depicts a
stylized bird.

99 An artistic
masterpiece, this
Aztec instrument is
a kind of flute in the
shape of a parrot. The
mouthpiece is at the
end of the long tail,
while the sound was
modulated by a hole
on the back and
emerged from the
beak.

musical instruments known to the
Mesoamerican world, but no texts
of musical notation have been found.
In the percussion section were tall,
leather-skinned single or double
drums known as *pax* in Mayan and
panhuehuetl in Nahuatl.

Another type of drum, the *teponaztli*,
was considered sacred by the Aztecs
and was also known to the Post-
Classic Maya. It probably originated
in Ecuador, but this is still debated.
Wind instruments included whistles,
ocarinas and simple flutes, and pan-
pipes, in wood or terra-cotta. Another
common instrument was made by the
Maya from the shells of sea turtles
and crustaceans. Various types of
trumpet were made of wood or
animal skin. Lastly, it seems that
stringed instruments remained
unknown until the Spanish Conquest.

Our historical and literary sources mention a number of forms of entertainment in addition to music and dance that were enjoyed by both the nobility and the population at large. A game of chance called *patolli* was the most popular among ordinary people. It was played in central Mexico and in the Maya territories as early as the Classic Period.

Descriptions of the game are contained above all in the Mixtec and Aztec codices, including the Codex Vindobonensis. Typically, *patolli* was not simply a means of passing time but was a kind of ritual with a precise and profound religious meaning. To play the game the equipment consisted of a surface painted on fabric and 12 counters in the form of small colored stones: six red and six blue. The cross-shaped board was subdivided into 52 squares along which the players moved their counters to reach the central square. Moves were made according to the throws of a kind of dice in the form of black beans with values painted white. The winner was the player (or pair of players) who managed to move his counters to the center of the cross first. According to the Spanish chroniclers, by the time of the Conquest *patolli* had become a complete obsession and was played at all hours in the streets of Tenochtitlan. Other, less popular, games included a kind of checkers using black and white pieces, and a game similar to present-day billiards.

The Aztecs also adopted sports from the peoples they subdued. Among these was the so-called "Voladores," the original Nahuatl name for which is unknown. In this spectacular demonstration of skill and courage, four men tied to strong ropes jumped from the top of poles, making a rapid spinning descent to the ground.

100–101 This scene, from the Codex Magliabechiano, illustrates one of the games most widely played by the subjects of Motecuhzoma, patolli. It was a game of chance and was extremely popular in central Mexico and in Maya regions.

101 (top) Another scene from the Codex Magliabechiano showing one of the adventurous sports practiced by the Aztecs. Brave young men climbed to the top of a tall pole before making a spinning descent to the ground, tied to a rope.

101 (right) This scene from the Codex Borbonicus shows a particular festivity that took place on the day of Xocotluetzi, dedicated to the god Huehueteotl. The young players had to climb to the top of a pole and grasp the emblem fixed there.

CRAFTS

Artifacts belonging to the various
civilizations of Pre-Columbian
Mesoamerica brought to light in
archaeological excavations bear
testimony to the extremely high levels
of skill achieved in various forms of
artistic expression from as early as the
Preclassic Period. Each culture
developed its own distinctive craft
products. These have been conserved
thanks above all to the practice of
placing in the tombs of the deceased a
range of objects that had accompanied
them during their lifetime.

Pottery production was probably the
most widespread craft activity. Vessels
of various forms and human and
animal figurines are common to all the
civilizations, but the most refined and
elegant examples are those produced
by the Maya during the Classic
Period. Numerous vessels
painted in bright colors illustrate
scenes of everyday life or

*102 (left) The
beautiful Mayan four-
footed pot shown here
comes from Tikal and
dates to the Classic
Period. It represents
a turkey, a bird
unknown in Europe
until the era of the
Spanish Conquest.*

*102 (above) In the
Classic Period the
Maya produced an
impressive range of
ceramics including
vessels decorated with
brightly colored
painted scenes. The
decoration of the bowl
seen here is a
depiction of a
dignitary, with a
series of glyphs.*

*102 (left) Animal
motifs appear
frequently in Maya
ceramics. This
sophisticated vessel
is painted with images
of parrots, and a head
of the same bird forms
the handle of the lid.
Certain birds such as
the parrot and the
hummingbird were
considered sacred by
Mesoamerican peoples.*

103 (above) A product of Aztec craft, this locust was found at Chapultepec. Although animal images are very common motifs in Mesoamerican art, those that were considered sacred or which had important roles in daily life were more frequently portrayed.

103 (right) This simple decorated bowl is incised with a fantastic animal that seems to combine human and monkey characteristics. It has been dated to the last centuries of the Maya culture.

103 (below) Maya pottery of the Classic Period was also used as a medium for writing. In the case of the cup shown here a series of glyphs describes the painted images.

mythological and religious themes. Figurines produced on the island of Jaina stand out for their fineness and details. In the tombs at Monte Albán, above all those of the Zapotec, unusual vessels equipped with covers and defined as "urns" are frequently found. These objects did not contain the ashes of the dead, however (who were buried rather than cremated), but probably had a votive function and depicted the divinities of the pantheon of Oaxaca.

Vessels of various types were made at Teotihuacan. Among these, two of the most unusual forms were covered censers and cylindrical tripod vases that were appreciated in and exported to other parts of Mesoamerica, in particular the Maya regions.

The ceramics produced in western Mexico are perhaps cruder, but their realistic style means they are extremely informative and they have provided precious information about aspects of these cultures that remained marginal compared with those of central Mexico.

The most widely used pottery technique was that of molding. It should be remembered that the potter's wheel remained unknown in the Americas until the Spanish Conquest.

105 (opposite) Also made of jade, the facial features of this frightening Mayan mask of a deity have been emphasized in relief and in red coloring. The eyes and the tongue are inlaid with shell. Until the Post-Classic Period the working of gold was unknown in Mesoamerica and jade was considered to be the most precious material.

104 All the peoples of Mesoamerica considered jade to be a precious material as it was associated with purity, water, and life. Jade was used to make exquisite jewelry and masks of great beauty, such as this pendant from Monte Albán. It depicts the bat god, whose terrible gaze is created by eyes of shell.

One of the oldest forms of Mesoamerican artistic expression was the carving of stones regarded as precious by the Mesoamerican people. The Olmecs, Maya, and the inhabitants of Teotihuacan excelled in the working of jade, serpentine, and obsidian, which they used to create funerary masks, statuettes, and a wide range of jewelry. Recent analysis has established that many objects long considered to be pure jade are in fact made of minerals such as diopside or chrysolite that are very similar to jade in color and hardness. The translucent green color of these stones was seen as symbolizing water, fertility, the sky, and vegetation. In all Mesoamerica, no other material was as precious as jade and the similar green stones. This was due both to their symbolic attributes and to their rarity and the difficulties of carving them.

Jade was usually found in the highlands and so had to be imported into areas where it was lacking. Moreover, the discovery of pieces larger than a river pebble was a very rare event. Wastage had to be kept to a minimum when cutting the stone, and the objects produced were handed down from generation to generation; in fact, in some jade objects in Mayan tombs date from the Olmec era.

106 Turquoise was first imported into Mesoamerica by the Toltecs, but it was Mixtec craftsmen who began to produce magnificent objects. Here a stunning mosaic of turquoise, obsidian, and pyrite covers a wooden mask.

107 (opposite above right) A magnificent example of mosaic art, this anthropomorphic figure was the handle of a sacrificial knife.

107 (opposite above left) This unusual wooden mask covered with a mosaic of pieces of turquoise, shell, and pyrite represents a deity. Although from the Aztec period, it is the work of a Mixtec craftsman, as are those that follow.

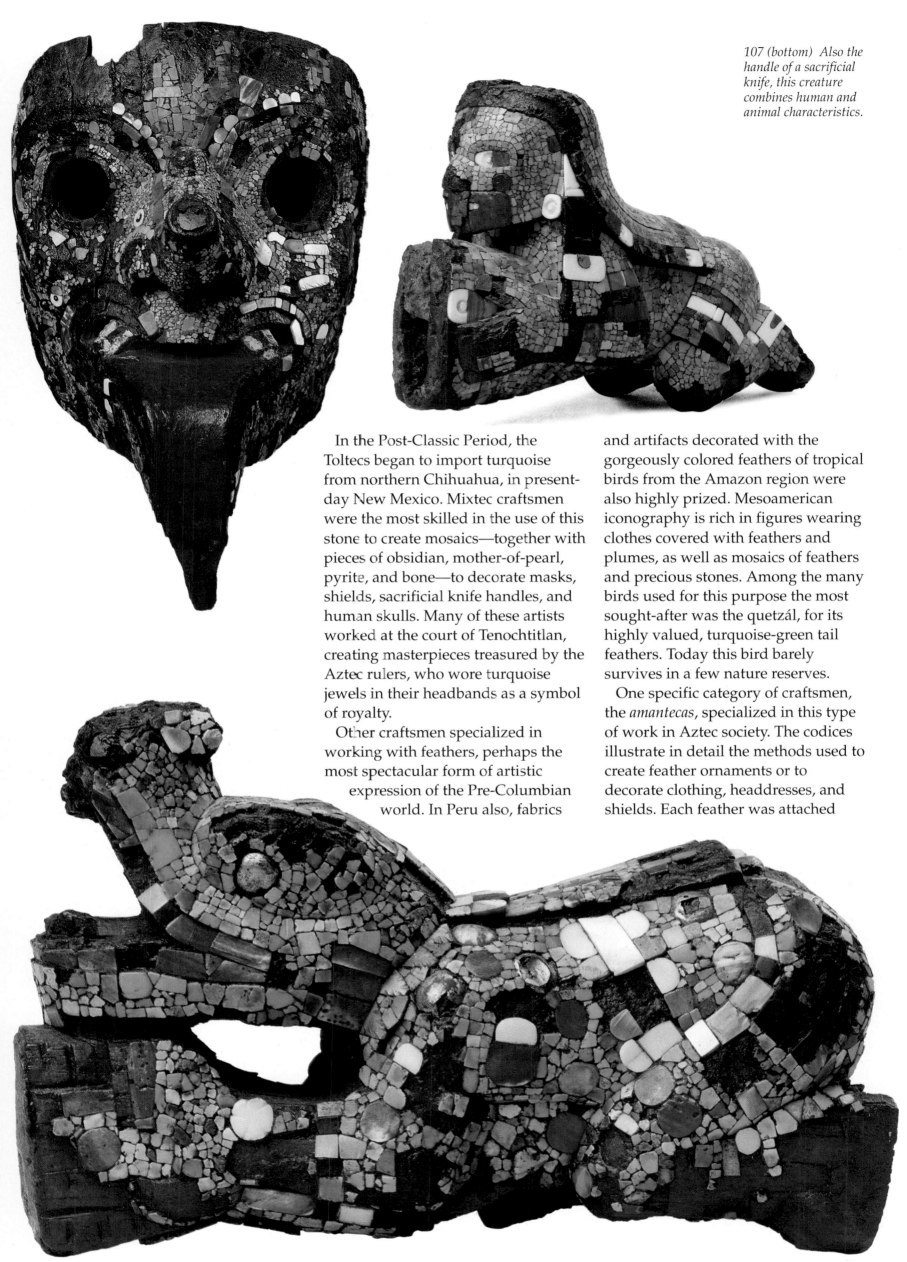

107 (bottom) Also the handle of a sacrificial knife, this creature combines human and animal characteristics.

In the Post-Classic Period, the Toltecs began to import turquoise from northern Chihuahua, in present-day New Mexico. Mixtec craftsmen were the most skilled in the use of this stone to create mosaics—together with pieces of obsidian, mother-of-pearl, pyrite, and bone—to decorate masks, shields, sacrificial knife handles, and human skulls. Many of these artists worked at the court of Tenochtitlan, creating masterpieces treasured by the Aztec rulers, who wore turquoise jewels in their headbands as a symbol of royalty.

Other craftsmen specialized in working with feathers, perhaps the most spectacular form of artistic expression of the Pre-Columbian world. In Peru also, fabrics and artifacts decorated with the gorgeously colored feathers of tropical birds from the Amazon region were also highly prized. Mesoamerican iconography is rich in figures wearing clothes covered with feathers and plumes, as well as mosaics of feathers and precious stones. Among the many birds used for this purpose the most sought-after was the quetzál, for its highly valued, turquoise-green tail feathers. Today this bird barely survives in a few nature reserves.

One specific category of craftsmen, the *amantecas*, specialized in this type of work in Aztec society. The codices illustrate in detail the methods used to create feather ornaments or to decorate clothing, headdresses, and shields. Each feather was attached with great delicacy using a thread of cotton to a reed or canvas backing to create extremely skillful and superbly colored mosaics. Costumes decorated with brilliant, iridescent feathers and birds' wings were worn during religious ceremonies and ritual dances.

In conclusion we will look at the last craft activity to be introduced to the Mesoamerican world, the working of metals. While in the countries of South America, the working of gold and silver was known from early times, it did not spread to Central America until the Post-Classic Period, with the Mixtec artists of Oaxaca.

Skilled craftsmen, the Mixtecs produced great quantities of jewelry, masks, breastplates, and gold and silver vessels using a range techniques: lost-wax casting, filigree,

108 (above) Part of the funerary treasure from Tomb 7 at Monte Albán, this gold pendant has iconography relating to the god Xipe-Totec, venerated in Oaxaca and also in the Aztec world. The style of the piece resembles the work of the goldsmiths of Ecuador and Colombia, from where techniques of working this metal came.

108 (left) The peoples of Pre-Columbian Mesoamerica and Peru excelled in the art of working with feathers. This Aztec shield depicts a coyote. A leather backing has been covered with feathers from quetzáls and flamingos, and gold threads.

and repoussé. The tombs of Monte Albán, of Zapotec origin but subsequently reused by the Mixtecs, contained great quantities of precious metals in the form of votive objects. Offerings found at the bottom of the Sacred Cenote at Chichén Itzá were equally rich.

Mixtec goldsmiths, like the workers in turquoise, were widely employed by the Aztec rulers; however, due to looting by the Conquistadores, very few precious metal objects from Tenochtitlan have survived to the present. The Aztec god of goldsmiths was Xipe-Totec, and the Nahuatl word for gold was *teocuitlatl*, "the excrement of the sun." But it is important to note that, in contrast with the Inca culture in which gold symbolized the sun and was therefore the most precious of materials, in the Mesoamerican world it never achieved the same status attributed to jade or quetzál feathers.

109 (left) On the occasion of ceremonies and festivals, the rulers and nobles of ancient Mesoamerica adorned themselves with sumptuous jewels and crowns, such as this one which must have belonged to a Mixtec dignitary.

109 (top) This sophisticated Mixtec gold breastplate was made using the techniques of filigree and embossing. It depicts a warrior whose chest is adorned with calendar glyphs.

109 In the Mesoamerican world necklaces, bracelets, and rings were not the only forms of jewelry worn. The tentetl, a nose or lip ornament, was also common. This precious gold example takes the form of an eagle's head.

109

Maya inscriptions of the Classic Period describe numerous wars and battles, exalting the feats of various rulers who extended the borders of their kingdoms or subdued neighboring city states and thus increased their own prestige. Reliefs carved on the stelae frequently illustrate scenes of the surrender of enemies to the victorious kings who would then reduce them to slavery or offer them as sacrifices to the gods.

We have numerous images of Maya warriors in the form of paintings and ceramic figurines, enabling us to reconstruct the military costumes worn during the period. Prior to combat, soldiers often wore a jaguar skin and mask, to absorb the strength and magical powers of the animal.

Maya shields were round and convex, more rarely rectangular. They would have been made of wood or leather, and those for ceremonial use were covered with a mosaic of precious stones or feathers. While we have only pictorial evidence for Maya shields, actual examples of elegant Aztec and Mixtec shields have been found, some of the latter still retaining traces of turquoise mosaics.

In the Classic Period the most commonly used weapon was a spear made of extremely hard wood and tipped with a sharpened point of obsidian or flint. Iron was introduced into Mesoamerica by the Europeans. In the Post-Classic Period, following the invasion of the Chichimecs, a new type of weapon was introduced to Mexico and successively adopted by the Mixtecs and the Aztecs—the bow and arrow, against which the soldiers protected themselves with special cotton-padded clothing. An ancient weapon was the spear-thrower, known as an *atlatl* in Nahuatl. The wooden sword tipped with obsidian was another commonly used weapon.

One curious detail of Maya war customs was the practice of dressing the hair of defeated enemies captured in battle in special styles. Prisoners were then decorated before being presented to the king, before whom they were obliged to perform an act of submission. The most warlike people of Mesoamerica were undoubtedly the Aztecs, the last of whose kings, once they had satisfied their expansionist aims and consolidated their borders, undertook a series of wars with the

111 *An informative illustration of the kind of military clothing worn during the Classic Period, this threatening terra-cotta warrior wears padded cotton armor, probably covered with feathers. From his back sprout two wings, perhaps a link with the warrior's totemic bird. He holds a rectangular shield in one hand, a rare shape among the Maya who preferred round shields. His ear disks, large necklace, and bracelet are also clearly visible.*

110 (opposite left) *A representation in ceramic of the torso of an Aztec warrior shows the typical protection worn in the period. This armor was made of padded cotton woven with feathers.*

110 (opposite above) *This cuirass of shell and mother-of-pearl found at Tula probably had a purely ritual function.*

110 (opposite below) *A Maya figurine possibly depicting a deity, holding a club in one hand and a round shield in the other. He wears long shin guards and a kind of protective breastplate.*

sole aim of capturing the greatest possible number of prisoners to sacrifice to Huitzilopochtli. These wars, fought constantly and known as the "Flower Wars," resulted in mass sacrifices, with the victims destined to feed the God of War with their blood so as to satisfy his terrible thirst and to ensure that the sun continued on its course. The prisoners were taken to the *temalacatl*, the sacrificial platform of stones at the top of temples where four priests immobilized the victim while a fifth opened his chest and offered the still beating heart to the gods. The Codex Mendoza illustrates scenes of battle

in which warriors drag prisoners by their hair who were to be taken alive to Tenochtitlan.

The military arts had a dominant role in the education of Aztec men, who from the age of fifteen were trained under the severest discipline. Once they reached adulthood there were no grounds for exemption from the military campaigns. Various military corps or societies existed, including the "Eagle Warriors" and the "Jaguar Warriors." There was also professional soldiers known as *quachictin*, the "shaven ones," who were always to be found in the most dangerous positions in battles and enjoyed great privileges.

112–113 (above) Many Maya images survive that relate to prisoners of war: one example is the carved relief scene on Stela 12 from Piedras Negras, which dates from the end of the Classic Period. This detail shows vanquished enemies tied together with a rope, with their hair knotted and pulled back, as a sign of their defeat and humiliation.

113 (left) This scene
from a Spanish
manuscript of the
Colonial era shows a
bloody battle of the
so-called "Flower
Wars," a form of
ritual warfare which
profoundly shocked
the Europeans.

113 (above) Dressed
in a simple loin-cloth,
this Jaina-style
figurine portrays a
warrior of noble and
elegant bearing. He
wears a ceremonial
headdress and a form
of face protection. In
his right hand he
holds a round shield,
decorated with
feathers.

DEATH AND BURIAL

Our knowledge of the ancient Mesoamerican civilizations owes much to the archaeological discovery of intact tombs and their contents. From the Preclassic Period on, members of the ruling elite were interred in subterranean tombs, generally beneath the floors of temple buildings. The extensive funerary treasures, which eased the deceased person's passage to the next world, constitute an essential source of information about the material culture and customs of the various peoples.

Among the civilizations that flourished in Oaxaca, the Gulf Coast of the Veracruz region, and in the Maya territories, inhumation was the most widespread funerary rite. The dead were wrapped in long mortuary cloths and a mask was placed over their faces. Perhaps the most celebrated examples of death masks have been found at Teotihuacan. In the Post-Classic Period, however, archaeology has shown that a fundamental change in funerary practice took place in certain areas. In contrast with other peoples, the Toltecs and the Aztecs practiced cremation: after wrapping the corpse in long bandages, it was burned and the ashes were buried together with copper axes.

Within the ceremonial center of Monte Albán, Zapotec dignitaries were buried in tombs around a patio and accessed via long staircases. Polychrome frescoes adorned the walls of the funerary chambers and niches housed the votive offerings to accompany the deceased into the next life. Also in the Oaxaca region, excavations in the cemetery of Mitla have revealed a series of cruciform-plan tombs beneath the floors of the ceremonial buildings.

The Mixtecs usually buried great quantities of gold and vessels as offerings with their deceased; along with such treasures the tombs also contained the remains of dogs and humans, the latter probably slaves sacrificed and buried to accompany the dead on their last journey.

Unusual funerary customs were also practiced by the cultures of western Mexico. In the 1st millennium BC, the Jalisco, Colima, and Nayarit peoples buried their dead in niches carved in solid rock, following a tradition originating in Ecuador. This, together with other cultural parallels, suggests that a series of contacts took place between the peoples of South and

114 A real human skull forms the base for a mosaic of turquoise and obsidian to create this terrifying mask associated with the fearsome Aztec god Tezcatlipoca, "Smoking Mirror." In the traditions of the Mexican peoples, Tezcatlipoca represented evil, the opposite of his brother Quetzalcoatl who was seen as an incarnation of goodness and the positive. Numerous victims were sacrificed in the name of Tezcatlipoca and their skulls were hung on racks or used, as in this case, to create cult objects.

115 (opposite) Death features frequently in Aztec art and perhaps no object better exemplifies this than this unusual skull carved with great skill from rock crystal. The god of death is also often depicted in Maya vase painting in macabre dances in the kingdom of the Underworld.

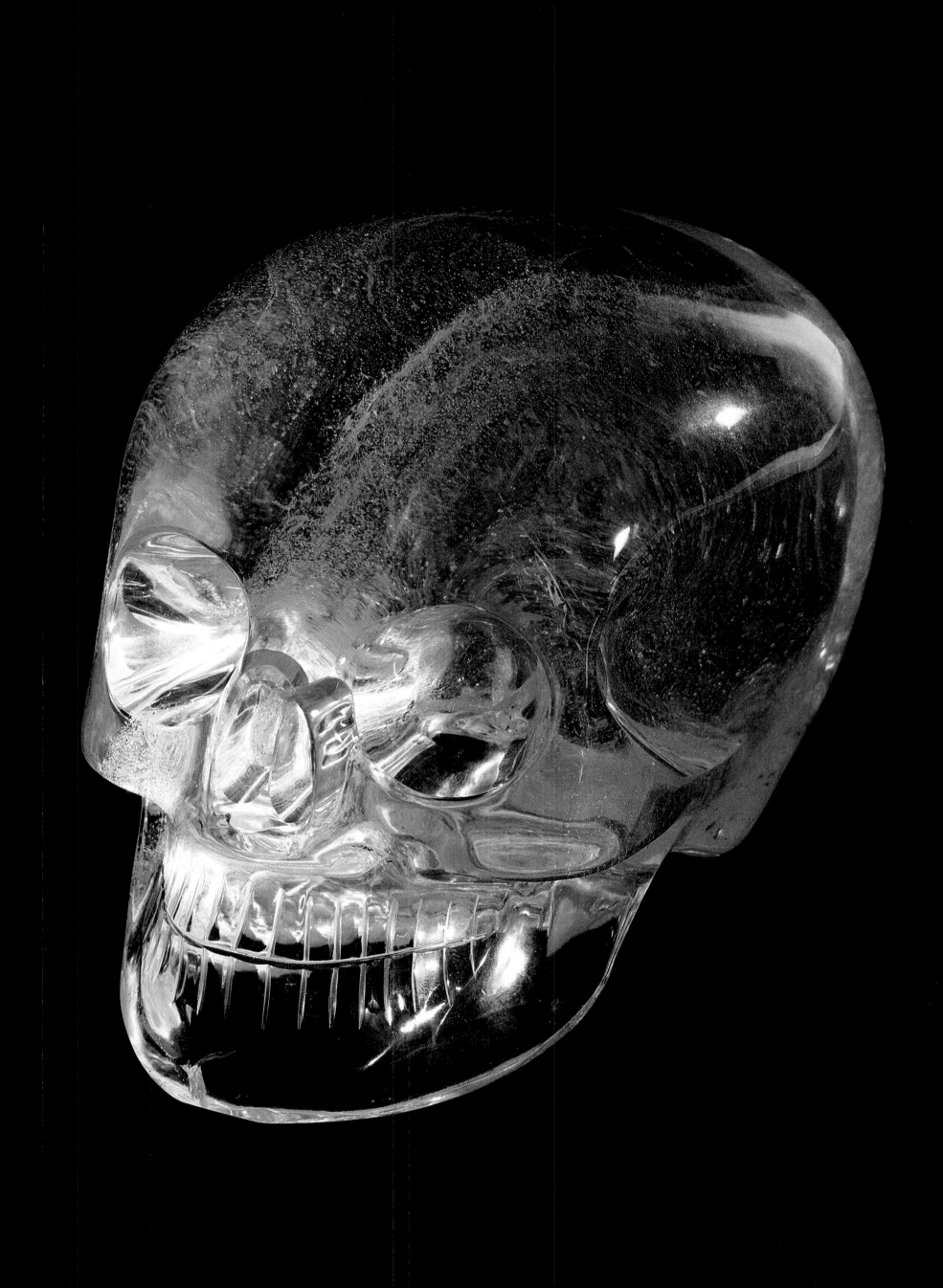

Central America in very early times. The tombs of western Mexico generally featured multiple chambers and it is presumed that the occupants of such tombs were all the members of the same family, buried together. Within these collective cemeteries numerous animal and human terracotta figurines have been found in the realistic and expressive local iconographical style. Rows of stones usually bounded the burial areas, perhaps designed to demarcate the world of the living from that of the dead.

Archaeology has uncovered a wealth of documentation on Maya funerary customs. Reviving an Olmec tradition, the Maya interred the bodies of high-ranking figures in large stone sarcophagi, and placed on and around the body jewels, masks of serpentine, feathers, fabrics, and various vessels. Priests and scribes were buried with their tools and instruments so that they could continue their work in the spiritual

116 (left) This colossal and rather stiff statue represents the Aztec goddess Coatlicue, "Serpent Skirt." Considered to be the mother of the Aztec tribal god Huitzilopochtli, this goddess was associated with the earth, darkness, and death, as indicated by her face, which has the appearance of a skull.

116 (above) Funerary masks, such as this one from Teotihuacan, were placed over the faces of the dead. The various peoples of Mesoamerica believed in a life after death and for this reason they filled the tombs of the deceased with rich funerary treasures, so they would lack for nothing on their final journey.

world. In many Maya cities of the Classic Period, the pyramidal temple buildings had a dual function. They were places of worship, but also burial mounds reserved for kings and dignitaries. The most famous and important example is the Temple of the Inscriptions at Palenque, the base of which concealed the great burial chamber of Lord Pacal.

Beautiful frescoes decorating the walls of the Río Azul tombs include a lexicon of symbols relating to the Maya religious and cosmogonic world. Rivers of water and blood flow in the Underworld, Xibalbá, as it is called in the sacred text the Popol Vuh.

Unfortunately, our information regarding the burial of the members of the lower classes is very scant. In the 16th century, the Spanish bishop Diego de Landa reported that the poorest families wrapped their dead in a kind of shroud and placed grains of maize or a bead of jade in their mouths to act as offerings and sustenance for their journey.

117 (below left) In the Classic Period images of skeletons dancing and performing special rituals frequently appear in art. This terra-cotta figurine was produced in the Veracruz region and portrays a skeleton in a seated position, its legs folded and its arms crossed. Its jaunty posture and bizarre headdress lend it an incongruously lively air.

117 (left) Three small, blue-painted quetzáls are modeled on the cover of this attractive vessel. It is a terra-cotta urn deposited as a votive offering in a Maya tomb of the Classic Period.

117 (below) In a scene taken from the Codex Magliabechiano figures perform rituals around a wrapped mummy placed on a kind of throne in an Aztec funeral ceremony.

The dead were buried near to or beneath the floor of their homes that were subsequently abandoned. The sumptuous funerary treasures of the nobility were replaced by simple figurines of clay and the tools of the deceased's trade. Landa also recorded another custom linked to the cult of the dead practiced in a restricted area of Yucatán. Here, in accordance with a tradition adopted from the Toltecs, the nobles were cremated and their ashes placed in hollows in the back of the heads of small statuettes in wood or terra-cotta. These anthropomorphic urns were not buried as they were in other areas, but were kept in the homes of the relatives and were venerated as ancestor idols.

Finally, it is interesting to consider the concept of death that these various Mesoamerican peoples developed. According to Aztec thought and tradition, life and death form a unified whole and their funeral rites, in contrast with those of European cultures past and present, had all the appearance of celebrations.

The Spanish monk Diego de Durán reported that in the 16th century, during the month of Tlaxochimaco, lengthy celebrations were held in honor of the children and adults who had died in the course of the previous year. In spite of the Christianization of the Mexican world, the concept of a "happy death" and related rituals did not disappear over the centuries, and still survive today alongside the usual Catholic rites. On the Day of the Dead in Mexico City and in the rural villages banquets accompanied by music and dancing are held in the cemeteries to allow the dead to participate once again in the joys of earthly life with their loved ones.

WRITING, ASTRONOMY, AND THE CALCULATION OF TIME

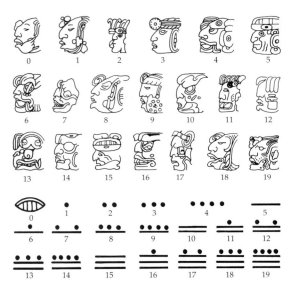

The oldest certain evidence of writing in Mesoamerica is to be attributed to the Zapotecs of Oaxaca and dates from 600 BC. Calendric glyphs have been identified on a number of stone monuments, but other symbols have yet to be deciphered. It is presumed, but not certain, that the Zapotec writing system derived from that of the Olmecs.

We also have evidence of the pictographic writing system of the Mixtecs, heirs to the Zapotec culture in the Post-Classic Period, in the form of a number of manuscript codices on deerskin. The symbols usually indicate names and dates relating to mythological or historical figures that appear in the painted scenes. In these texts, therefore, the pictorial elements carry the narrative.

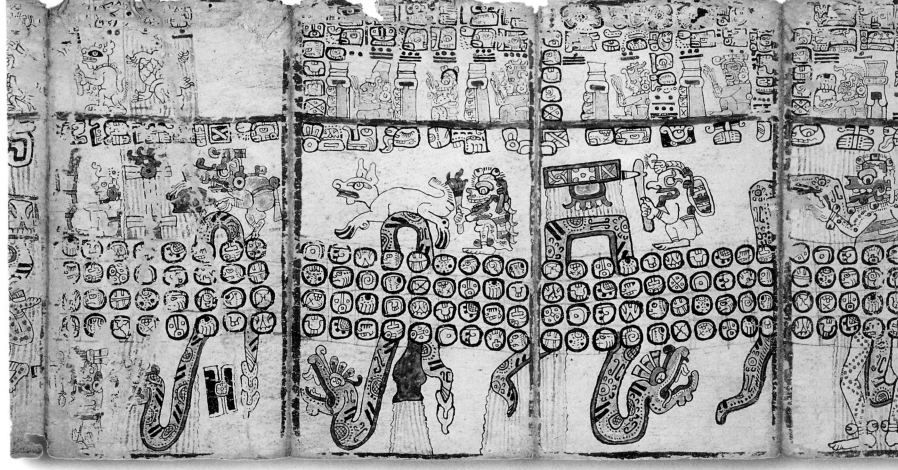

118 (above left) This diagram illustrates the Maya system of indicating numbers from 1 to 19. The dot represents one unit and a bar the number 5. The number 20 was expressed with the glyph of the moon and zero with that of a shell. Each figure could also be indicated with a sign known as the pictorial variant.

118 (top right) Maya glyphs were often incorporated in pottery decoration, as on this pretty terra-cotta tankard from Uaxactún.

118–119 (above) Images of deities and painted glyphs decorate this fragment of one of the four known Maya codices, the Madrid Codex.

Two objects from the Veracruz region carry traces of another system of writing with a more complex structure than that of the Zapotecs: Stela 1 of La Mojarra and the Tuxtla Statuette, dating from around the 2nd century BC. Both objects are inscribed with text written in a mixed idiom—composed of pictographic and phonetic glyphs. They have been deciphered and seem to relate to a language from the Mixe-Zoquean family, to which, according to some

experts, the Olmec language also belongs. Due to the restricted sources it is therefore still difficult to place this writing system in a precise cultural context, but it is probably safe to say that it was of Olmec derivation.

A writing system of the same kind, composed of pictograms and phonetic symbols, was adopted and revised by the Maya of the lowlands. In the Classic Period epigraphic texts are frequently found accompanying the carved images on reliefs, as well on pottery and in wall paintings. These are fundamentally historical accounts designed to glorify the lives of the ruling families, accompanied by calendric references. This rich narrative archive only began to be deciphered from the 1960s, thanks to the painstaking work of Russian, American and European epigraphists.

Only four Maya codices, dating from the Post-Classic Period, survived the deliberate destruction ordered by the Spanish bishop Diego de Landa. These codices consist of numerous pages made of agave or fig bark fiber, folded and painted with divinatory, religious, and astronomical scenes and texts. Although they were compiled just a few centuries before the Conquest, the authors of the codices probably drew on older sources.

Scholars are still exploring the origins of this knowledge and the instruments used to acquire it. One suggestion is that the stimulus constantly to observe astral phenomena and to use those observations to organize the passage of time was born out the needs of a prevalently agricultural society whose economy and wealth were based on the products of the land. For the people of Mesoamerica it was of fundamental importance to predict, on the basis of their astronomical observations, events such as floods and drought. Other suggestions have been put forward, but at present there remain a great number of unanswered questions.

119 The Maya writing system is in part pictographic and in part phonetic. Texts are found on various materials including stone, sheets of vegetable fiber, bone, ceramic, and jade. Maya glyphs form elaborate miniatures enclosed within scrolls and are composed of various symbols which are read differently according to the context. The three glyphs shown below all come from Palenque.

A larger number of Aztec codices, including the marvellously detailed Codex Mendoza, survive. Rich sources of historical and mythological information, they reveal a keen interest in the passage of time and a highly developed knowledge of astronomy—knowledge that also reached impressive heights under the Maya. Studying the movements of heavenly bodies and calendric computations implies also considerable mathematical skills.

The Maya were certainly the greatest astronomers and mathematicians of Mesoamerica, as the stone inscriptions and surviving codices demonstrate. They achieved a detailed level of knowledge of the sun, the cycles of the moon, and the movements of a number of planets in the solar system, especially Venus but probably also Jupiter, Mars, Mercury, and Saturn.

The Paris Codex and the Dresden Codex, the most complete and oldest of the texts, contain many pages illustrating the cycle of Venus which was thought of not as a planet but perhaps the most important star in the heavens in its dual role of "Evening Star" and "Morning Star." Venus was associated with the concept of war and was personified as a magnificent warrior. Solar eclipses were seen as phenomena of great importance and were well described in the pages of the Dresden Codex. The Maya were aware of the movements of the constellations and regarded the Pole Star as particularly important as it was the guiding light of travelers and merchants.

The Milky Way was known as Zac Beh, "the White Road," in the Yucatec language and was considered by the Maya to be the road along which the spirits slid to reach Xibalbá, the Underworld. Several deities were associated with the Milky Way, the most famous being Mixcoatl, the Toltec god known as "Cloud Serpent." A page, unfortunately fragmentary, in the Paris Codex depicts a number of figures which originally composed a zodiac.

As with all the elements making up the Cosmos, the sun, the moon, the planets and the stars were identified as divine beings. Classic Period inscriptions inform us that ceremonies, wars, and sacrifices took place only after the astral conjunctions had been examined.

Mesoamerican astronomers performed their duties in purpose-built constructions, of which the "Caracol" at Chichén Itzá is possibly one. Glass and lenses were unknown in Pre-Columbian America and the surviving images suggest that the instruments used consisted of a pair of crossed canes: the positions and movements of the stars were noted in relation to notches in the wood.

Maya mathematical calculations used a vigesimal system, that is one based on the number 20, almost certainly inherited from the Zapotecs. The numbers from one to 19 were expressed with a system of dots and bars or by the heads of mythological monstrous beings. The symbol of the moon was used to indicate the number 20. One perhaps surprising element was the "discovery" of the concept of zero many centuries before the Hindu mathematicians of the Old World.

120 This jadeite pendant, both sides of which are shown here, is known as the "Leiden Plate" after the Dutch city where it is now kept. It is an unusual as well as a beautiful object, due in particular to its meaning. One side is inscribed with elaborate iconography with the image of a Maya lord trampling a captive underfoot, who has been identified as a king of Tikal. On the other face is a calendric inscription with the Long Count date corresponding to AD 320.

121 (opposite) A detail of Stela 31 from Tikal. The inscriptions narrate the story of one of the most famous lords to have ruled the city, Stormy Sky. At the end of the 1950s the Maya inscriptions had yet to be deciphered, but then the epigraphist Tatiana Proskouriakoff succeeded in decoding the signs beginning with the calendric symbols, showing that the Maya had left a series of epigraphic historical documents as well as the divinatory texts found in their codices.

GODS AND RELIGION

The Mesoamerican religious pantheon is vast and extremely complex. Gods and goddesses are depicted in stone reliefs, pottery decoration, and wall paintings, and in the various Maya, Aztec, and Mixtec codices from the Post-Classic Period. Many of these deities are common to the various civilizations and their worship survived over time, frequently taking on different characteristics in different areas. It is important to bear in mind that the Mesoamerican concepts of "god" and "religion" cannot be compared with those of the Old World. For the Mesoamerican peoples, everything, every element of the Cosmos, the earth on which humans live, the sun, the moon, the stars, and everything that forms part of nature —animals, plants, water, and mountains—were all "divine" and all represented a manifestation of the supernatural.

From the Preclassic Period onward, a series of cults linked to various aspects of natural elements developed in all the Mesoamerican cultures. Traces of these cults have survived in the iconography of various art forms. Cults connected with the jaguar and with jade were found throughout Mesoamerica. Jade, with its translucent green color was venerated together with water as a symbol of life and fertility. Curiously, jade has always been an object of veneration in China for the same reason. Another ancient cult was that related to mountains and caves. Great masks with gaping jaws and monstrous features in stone or stucco were located at the entrance to many Olmec and Maya temples, symbolizing the caverns and caves on the flanks of the mountains that allowed access to the depths of Mother Earth and the shadowy roads that led to the

Underworld, called Xibalbá in the sacred Maya text, the Popol Vuh.

Here, we have space to discuss only the most significant of the deities worshiped by the diverse civilizations that flourished in the Mesoamerican area. Despite differences of chronology or geography, the essential aspects of this religious pantheon were shared by all the peoples, born out of a common cultural foundation. The idea of a supreme creator god was handed down to the Maya and the Aztecs in the form of, respectively, Itzamná and Ometeotl. Both of these deities embodied the concept of

122 (opposite) Mesoamerican art is incredibly rich in images associated with various deities of the religious pantheon, some of whom, like the goddess of the moon and the god of rain, were venerated by all the civilizations, while others were more regional. This terra-cotta sculpture represents the god Huehueteotl, considered by the Aztecs to be the "Old God." His cult and iconography dated back to ancient times.

123 (above) This sculpture also represents the "Old God," Huehueteotl, whose iconography is common to many parts of Mesoamerica. This deity is usually depicted, as in this piece from Veracruz, with the features of an old, hunched man, sitting with his legs crossed and his hands on his knees. His eyes are half-closed, almost as if to suggest the onset of blindness.

dualism—that is to say a supernatural being that was both positive and negative, male and female.

As with many ancient peoples all over the world, special veneration was reserved for the god of the sun, which represented the star of life and light. The Maya name for this god was Kinich Ahau, meaning "Great Sun Lord." In his nocturnal aspect he was represented as the jaguar god: the sun hidden from the eyes of man. For the Aztecs, and probably the Toltecs too, the sun god was called Tonatiuh. He was depicted with his head crowned by an eagle, the symbol of power, and by the solar disk emanating rays. The male deity of the sun was complemented by the female goddess of the moon. Among the Maya of the Classic Period she was represented by

a young woman, a symbol of the moon in its waxing phase, sitting on a crescent moon holding a rabbit. In the Mixtec and Aztec codices the moon was also associated with this animal as the Mesoamerican people believed that in its mottled surface could be made out the profile of a rabbit's head.

In the Post-Classic Period the iconography of the young woman disappeared and, according to certain scholars, the cult of the moon was absorbed by that of the ancient goddess Ixchel, who was connected with medicine and female fertility. The corresponding Aztec moon goddess was perhaps Coyolxauhqui, but this is not certain.

As the Mesoamerican peoples obtained most of their food through

Maize, the principal agricultural crop, also had its tutelary deity. For the Maya this was Yum Yac, of ancient origin and depicted as a young man with fine features and a maize plant on his head. No similar images have been found in central Mexico that pre-date the late Post-Classic Period when various male deities linked to maize and agriculture were found, among whom the most important was probably Cinteotl.

Apart from those mentioned, innumerable other deities were also venerated. Frequently they are difficult to identify due to the scarcity of, or contradictions in, our sources.

125 (center) This unusual stone figurine is a tecalli, a ceremonial object representing a "solar dart." According to Sahagún, such objects were used by the priests to enable them to "see the spirits of men."

125 (below) The rather rigid and formal figure in polychrome terra-cotta seen here represents the Aztec god Nappatecuhtli, whose name means something like "Four Times Lord." Some aspects of the iconography of this god recall the god of rain, Tlaloc. The Aztecs imported this cult from the southern regions of Mexico.

agriculture, the most feared and venerated deity was perhaps the god of rain and water. Drought signified disaster and death, while life and wealth depended absolutely on the god of rain. Iconography relating to this god, again under different names, can be found throughout Mesoamerica. For the Zapotecs of Oaxaca he was Cocijo, while in central Mexico from the Classic Period onward the god was known as Tlaloc. Teotihuacan may have been a center of the cult of this agricultural deity, a cult that was probably inherited by the Toltecs and the Aztecs. One of the twin sanctuaries at the top of the Templo Mayor in Tenochtitlan was dedicated to Tlaloc. To the Maya the god of rain and lightning was Chac, whose characteristic iconography, with a long, curling nose dates from the Preclassic Period. After AD 1000, following the Toltec invasion, the cult of the Sacred Cenote was established at Chichén Itzá and other centers in the Yucatán. The Cenote was a kind of natural well into which victims were thrown as offerings to Chac. Those who survived and clambered out of the murky waters delivered responses and predictions from the god.

125 (above left) This Aztec female statuette represents a kneeling goddess or priestess adorned with jewels. On her face can be seen signs of ritual scarification, a common practice among Mesoamerican peoples.

125

Among those worthy of special notice are the god of war and the god of death, represented by the Aztecs as the figures of Tezcatlipoca and Huitzilopochtli, and the god of merchants and cacao, particularly venerated by the Maya. After the year AD 1000, the Toltec invaders of the Yucatán, who brought with them their own culture to the Maya cities of the region, also imported a "foreign" cult, the history and origins of which are still the subject of much research. Quetzalcoatl, the Nahuatl name of the god, means "Feathered Serpent." In the Maya-Yucatec language he was known as Kukulcan. A mysterious serpent-like figure, this god was covered with the emerald feathers of the sacred quetzál.

Although this cult flourished during the Post-Classic Period with the rise of the Toltec people, the iconography of the hybrid serpent-bird creature has distant origins, dating back to the Olmec civilization. Monument 19 at La Venta has an image of a serpent with the beak and crest of a bird. Subsequently, during the Classic Period, images of the Feathered Serpent appeared in Veracruz and at Copán, in the form of decorative motifs, and at Teotihuacan where, in the 3rd century AD an important temple was dedicated to the god.

In the centuries leading up to the Spanish Conquest, the cult of the Feathered Serpent became pre-eminent throughout the regions of Mexico influenced initially by the Toltecs and then subjected to the dominion of the Aztecs. In the Aztec and Maya codices of the Post-Classic Period, Quetzalcoatl-Kukulcan is depicted as a flesh-and-blood being and identified as the patron of wind, medicine, and the arts. In one tradition the mythical light-skinned,

126 (top) Among the cults found in Mesoamerica, that of Quetzalcoatl, the Feathered Serpent—seen here in an Aztec sculpture—is one of the most complex and enigmatic. The iconography associated with the god was present in the Preclassic Period but spread above all with the rise of the Toltecs.

126 This relief comes from the Temple of the Eagles at Chichén Itzá. It depicts a jaguar in the act of devouring a human heart. The iconography of the jaguar is found in Mesoamerican art in many forms. In this particular example the jaguar god has been associated by the Toltecs with death and sacrifice.

127 (top and bottom) The principal deities of the Aztec pantheon are represented in the codices. These images, from the Florentine Codex of Sahagún, depict a number of gods and their attributes.

bearded figure of Quetzalcoatl was dethroned by his evil brother Tezcatlipoca, the Aztec god of war, and fled to the Gulf of Mexico where he burst into flames and ascended to the heavens, transformed into the Morning Star, or Venus. In another version the god sailed away across the sea on a raft of serpents, promising that he would return. The Aztec king Motecuhzoma II may have been misled by this legend into identifying Hernán Cortés as the bearded god.

127 (center) This image of Quetzalcoatl is also from the Florentine Codex. The Aztecs and other peoples of the Post-Classic Period superimposed the figure of the Feathered Serpent over other sacred figures. He was therefore venerated as the god of wind, the arts, and the sciences, taking on the role of supreme creator and civilizing god.

SACRIFICE AND AUTOSACRIFICE

128 (below) This Aztec stone casket was intended to contain votive offerings made to the gods. These would have varied according to the context and the economic means of those making the offering. Inside the cover is the symbol of the "Center of the Universe."

In the religious panorama of Pre-Columbian Mesoamerica sacrificial rites had a fundamental role. The purpose of sacrifice was to offer a gift to the gods and the most precious gift was blood, considered to be the regenerative essence of life.

Archaeological evidence shows that from the earliest times animals and human beings were sacrificed to feed the gods, to thank them, or to placate their wrath in times of famine and drought. To the Maya the supreme sacrificial animal was the jaguar, which embodied divine strength, but dogs, hummingbirds, and turkeys were also sacrificed. All kinds of ceremony were accompanied by sacrifices: calendric festivals, coronations and royal marriages, dedicatory rituals for buildings, and astronomical events.

Moreover many Mesoamerican peoples performed autosacrifice. This was a form of ritual bloodletting from wounds self-inflicted to various parts of the body. Mayan reliefs and inscriptions of the Classic Period describe this chilling ritual: the rulers and their wives, or the priests and shamans, drew blood from themselves with sharp instruments such as obsidian knives and agave spines. This practice, together with dancing and drug-taking induced a trance-like state and hallucinatory visions that represented the interface between this world and the Underworld. Self-sacrifice was also intended to feed the earth with life-blood and thus ensure an abundant crop of maize.

In the Post-Classic Period, many cities but in particular Tula and Chichén Itzá, contain chacmools. These stone sculptures took the form of a recumbent man, holding a receptacle for offerings, perhaps sometimes human hearts.

Written accounts report that in the last phase of the Aztec empire, in order to satisfy the god Huitzilopochtli, thousands of prisoners were sacrificed at the Templo Mayor in Tenochtitlan in a single day. The smell of the blood that coated the walls and stairway of the temple was so strong that the nobles had to hold nosegays to their noses. This custom aroused the hatred of the subject peoples and undermined the very foundations of the empire itself.

128 (opposite left below) Lintel 24 from Yaxchilán is carved with a relief scene of autosacrifice. Lord Shield Jaguar stands in front of his wife Lady Xoc who is piercing her tongue with a cord threaded with spines in order to offer her blood and induce a hallucinatory state.

128 (opposite right above) The peoples of Mesoamerica practiced sacrificial rituals to feed the gods with blood. One of the instruments used by the Aztecs was the tecpatl, a sacred sacrificial knife associated with the cult of the god Xipe-Totec. Two examples are shown here in the form of flint blades, adorned with shell and obsidian fragments.

129 (above) Chacmools are found throughout Mesoamerica, from the end of the Classic Period on, but in particular at Tula and Chichén Itzá. These sculptures take the form of a man lying on his back with his legs folded up. The receptacle on the chest held offerings, perhaps even human hearts.

129 (right) Diego de Durán provides a horrifying account of human sacrifices performed by the Aztecs. This illustration from his Historia de las Indias shows priests cutting open the chest of a victim held down on a sacrificial altar.

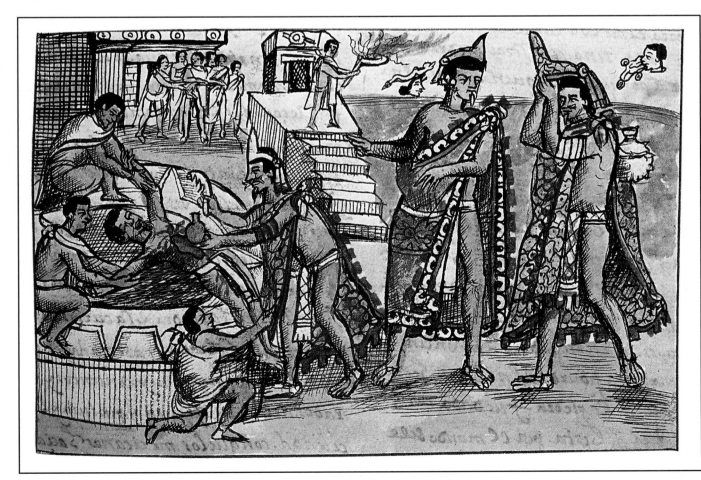

SACRED ARCHITECTURE

Religion and worship had a dominant role in lives of the people of ancient Mesoamerica and the representatives of civil power were also considered as divine beings. As a reflection of this, temples and tombs are among the principal architectural monuments in Mesoamerica.

Temples—*nah*, "edifice," in Mayan and *teocalli* in Aztec Nahuatl—were at the heart of the cities. The oldest temple buildings date to the middle of the Preclassic Period, belonging to the Olmec culture. All the principal Mesoamerican centers such as Monte Albán, Teotihuacan, Palenque, Tikal, El Tajín, Chichén Itzá, and many others were dominated by pyramidal temples, some of which were of enormous size. Their form was a symbolic reference to a mountain, where mere mortals could approach the gods. Mountains, *witz* to the Maya and *tepetl* in central Mexico, were the objects of an ancient cult found not only in Mesoamerica, but also among many of the peoples of pre-Inca Peru.

A number of temples in the Olmec and Maya territories also featured monstrous masks with gaping jaws at the entrances. These symbolized the caverns that were considered magical sites. Others, such as the ancient fluted pyramid at La Venta, probably symbolized volcanoes.

The true site of worship, the sanctuary where the

priests and members of the elite performed ceremonies, sacrifices, and rituals, was located at the summit of the pyramid and was reached by a steep stairway. During the ceremonies and festivals, the general public remained at the base of the temple. In some cases no traces of the sanctuaries have survived, as they were built of perishable materials.

Many rulers, like the famous Lord Pacal of Palenque, were buried in or beneath the temples so that their bodies would rest peacefully within the sacred building. The temple was never an isolated structure within the vast ceremonial centers and cities. It was almost always set within an architectural complex consisting of plazas, ball courts, and grandiose buildings that today are often simply labeled "palaces" but which probably had multiple functions, undoubtedly integrated with those of the temple. The various elements that together formed these ceremonial complexes were not placed at random but were

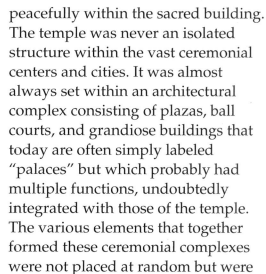

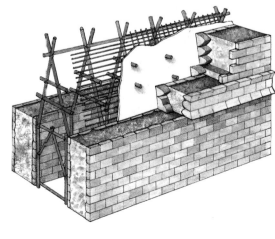

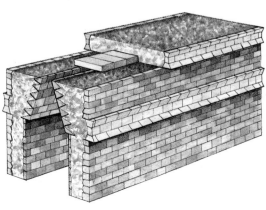

130 (opposite left above) A common architectural element that originated at Teotihuacan but subsequently spread throughout Mesoamerica was the talud-tablero system shown in this drawing. It consisted of a vertical panel, the tablero, placed over a sloping wall, the talud.

130 (opposite right above) Although only the foundations of many temples have survived, a number of clay models, such as the one seen here, have been found.

130 (opposite left below) Known as the "Monument of Sacred War" or the "Temple Stone," this basalt sculpture was dedicated on the occasion of the ceremony of the New Fire in 1507 as an emblem of Aztec supremacy in the Valley of Mexico. Probably a throne, it takes the form of a miniature temple.

130–131 (left) Aztec and Mixtec codices illustrate a number of forms of sacred architecture. This page from a Mixtec codex from Oaxaca of the Colonial era shows some stylized temples.

131 (below) The Mesoamerican peoples did not have the true arch but used the "false arch" or corbeling technique instead. As shown in this drawing, this involved each successive course projecting slightly beyond the one below until a narrow gap at the top was capped by horizontal slabs.

often oriented according to the cardinal points.

In addition to temples, some pyramidal structures had a particular role linked to the passage of time and the calendric cycles; one example is the Pyramid of the Niches at El Tajín. Others had features linked to precise cosmogonic references; Temple I at Tikal and the Temple of the Inscriptions at Palenque were built on nine levels, symbolising the nine levels of the Underworld. Yet other buildings with unusual architectural

132–133 The shape of the Mesoamerican temple symbolized the concept of the mountain, considered sacred as it allowed man to approach the gods. The oldest temples date back to the Olmecs and temple architecture evolved through the centuries, gradually becoming more elaborate. This drawing, reproducing Piedras Negras, in Guatemala, shows the various elements of temple architecture in the Classic Period.

The acropolis was composed of a series of platforms crossed by great stairways. At the summit were courts or "plazas," usually rectangular in shape, residential buildings, and the actual temples in the form of stepped pyramids. The highest point was occupied by the sanctuary, which was often crowned with a roofcomb. The whole structure was painted in bright colors or covered with polychrome stucco.

features or forms have tentatively been identified as astronomical observatories. Among these, the best known are Building J at Monte Albán, the Caracol at Chichén Itzá, the Tower of the Palace at Palenque, and the Palace of the Governor at Uxmal. As already noted, the observation of the stars and the interpretation of celestial phenomena were important elements in Mesoamerican culture and were closely linked to cosmogony and religion. Seen in this context, therefore, the observatories can also be thought of as "sacred" buildings. Illustrations showing observatories built by the Aztecs and the Mixtecs

(of which no physical traces remain) have been found in certain codices and paintings. In the Aztec capital Tenochtitlan, the temple buildings were usually flanked by residences reserved for the members of the priesthood and by theological schools. Lastly, Mesoamerican religious architecture was completed by the ball court, the area devoted to the ritual ball game.

It should also be remembered that, as far as is known, the true arch was not used in Mesoamerica. All the vaulted spaces that have survived were built using the so-called "false arch" or corbeling technique.

THE BALL GAME

134 (below) Ball players were depicted by all Mesoamerican civilizations. This terra-cotta figurine from western Mexico is a product of the Colima culture and portrays a player equipped with a helmet and a protective belt.

The ball game can be considered as the oldest ritual sport of Mesoamerica and is still played in north-western Mexico. Its origins are probably to be found in the Gulf Coast region and date back to the 1st millennium BC, the Olmecs being the first people to observe that the latex collected from the rubber tree bounced. A simple, early ball court has been found at the Olmec site of San Lorenzo and the presence of courts all over Mesoamerica testifies to the importance of a ritual that was still practiced by the Aztecs up to the Spanish Conquest.

Most ball courts consisted of an arena surrounded by stone walls forming a capital letter "I" in plan, subdivided into two well-defined parallel zones. Spectators, who regularly bet on the outcome of the game, sat along the longer side on stepped terraces. Two massive stone rings were fixed to the side walls at a considerable height from the ground, usually at the half-way mark of the court.

The game was played between two teams, each composed of two or three players, all belonging to the nobility and all male.

Images of women have been found in connection with the ball game only at one site, Yaxchilán.

Players had to direct a heavy, solid rubber ball into their opponents' half of the court without letting it bounce in their own half. They were not allowed to touch the ball with their hands or feet, but used their heads, thighs, and knees. These parts were protected by straps of padded deerskin to absorb the violent impact of a ball weighing up to several kilos. The highest score was obtained by getting the ball through your opponents' ring, although the precise rules of the game varied from place to place.

134 (opposite top right)
134 (opposite top right) Poised for the ball game, a player with an athletic and majestic bearing wears a protective belt and other equipment. This beautiful Mayan figurine is from Guatemala.

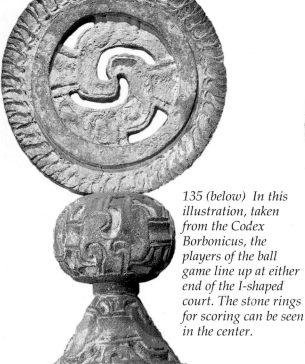

135 (below) In this illustration, taken from the Codex Borbonicus, the players of the ball game line up at either end of the I-shaped court. The stone rings for scoring can be seen in the center.

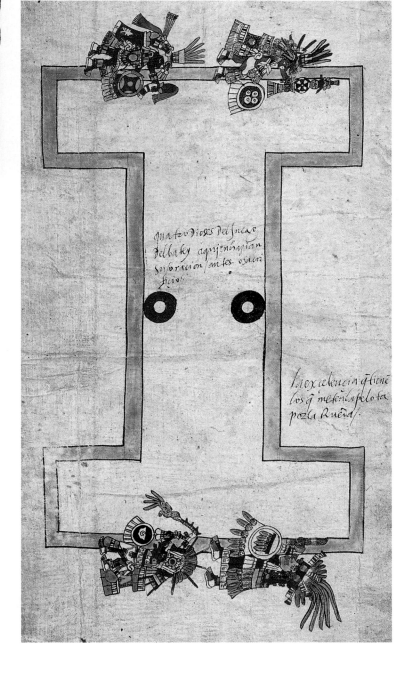

135 (above) This unusual object comes from Teotihuacan and acted as a boundary stone marking out the court for the ritual ball game.

135 (above right) A ball player is depicted in relief in the center of this commemorative stone disc. The long spiral inscription around the design contains a date corresponding to AD 590.

More than a simple sport, the game also had great religious significance. The movement of the ball reflected that of the sun, and the players had the symbolic role of "supporters" of the solar disk in its passage through day and night and were charged with the task of ensuring that it never fell to earth. The game could last for days and the members of the losing team were in some instances decapitated as they had failed to support the sun.

For the Maya the ball game was closely tied to the practice of human sacrifice. In the Classic Period, the players might be prisoners of war or slaves: at the end of the game the losers were tied and bound to become the "ball," and were thrown along the terracing. Equally gruesome was a Post-Classic Maya tradition: the winners decapitated the losers and hung their heads on skull racks.

Countless ball courts have been found in Mesoamerica differing in structure and size. However, in the Veracruz region in particular, the ritual ball game was of great importance: the number of courts and objects relating to the game such as the stone "yokes," "hachas," and "palmas" suggest that championships were held, attended by people from throughout the region.

ARCHAEOLOGICAL ITINERARIES IN MESOAMERICA

138–139 One of the chacmools of Chichén Itzá, at the top of the staircase of the Temple of the Warriors. This figure is perhaps the emblem of the Maya-Toltec civilization that flourished at this site in the Yucatán in the Post-Classic Period.

THE DISCOVERY OF LOST WORLDS

The civilizations that succeeded one another in Mesoamerica over the centuries up to the European Conquest have left numerous traces of their passing in the form of architectural remains, the beauty and scale of which still astonish visitors. It is therefore easy to comprehend the surprise and wonder felt by the travelers and explorers who, in the 18th and 19th centuries, witnessed the spectacle presented by the rediscovered ruins of the strange and

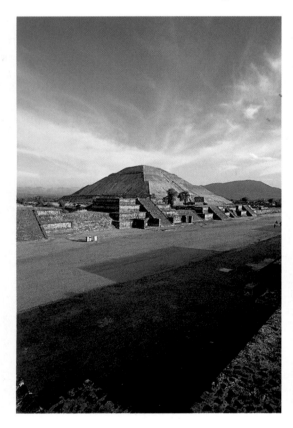

majestic buildings constructed by the Maya in a remote past. Abandoned for centuries, for the most part they were engulfed in dense tropical vegetation.

Among these travelers were the American lawyer John Stephens and the painter Frederick Catherwood. Between 1836 and 1850 Catherwood undertook several journeys in Maya regions, discovering numerous sites that he recorded in meticulous drawings and watercolours. For the first time, the existence of civilizations with ancient roots and mysterious features was revealed to the eyes of a westerner who, with memories of the

Conquest long faded, began a "curious and scientific" exploration of those distant times and exotic lands.

Today, after years of archaeological research, it has been shown that many ceremonial centers and cities disappeared as a result of natural catastrophes such as volcanic eruptions and earthquakes; others were abandoned after invasion, famine, or unknown causes. The most striking example is Tenochtitlan, the fabulous Aztec capital of which only a few ruins survived the destructive greed and fury of the Spanish under Hernán Cortés.

138 (above left) Teotihuacan was founded during the Preclassic Period, and over the course of the centuries was transformed into a true metropolis. The Pyramid of the Sun, which can be seen here, is the largest temple building in Mexico after that at Cholula. The temple was built over a cave, the design and remains of which suggest that it was a sanctuary dedicated to the cult of spring waters.

138–139 (above) The Castillo at Chichén Itzá is a massive pyramidal structure with a square base. Four stairways, one on each side, provide access to the sanctuary at the top. The temple visible today was built over an older and smaller structure. This building was never demolished and is still beneath the more recent temple.

139 (bottom left) Building J at Monte Albán was constructed by the Zapotecs in the Preclassic Period. It is aligned with the star Capella and may have been an astronomical observatory.

139 (bottom right) Traces of color are still visible on the atlantean pillars of the temple at Toltec Tula. These gigantic statues once supported the roof of the sanctuary on top of the platform.

Having examined the principal
aspects of the ancient Mesoamerican
civilizations, their history, and culture,
we can now undertake an
archaeological tour of the traces that
remain—the temples, "palaces," and
other monuments that were symbols
of the religious and civic power of the
cities that rose and fell over the course
of time. The journey begins in the area
where, in the second millennium

before Christ, the Mesoamerican
peoples built the first great stone
buildings in a context of rural villages:
the tropical region of Veracruz-
Tabasco, along the Gulf of Mexico.
Here, the Olmecs founded the oldest
ceremonial centers of Mesoamerica,
among which the most imposing was
undoubtedly that of La Venta. Today,
the monuments of La Venta are
displayed in the archaeological park
at Villahermosa.

Although many of its aspects are
still unknown, it seems that Olmec
culture was never completely lost,
rather it was inherited by successive
civilizations. The Villahermosa park
contains some of the most instantly
recognizable symbols of ancient
Mexico: colossal basalt heads
featuring distinctive physical traits.

Our itinerary continues to what
were the principal centers of the
Oaxaca region: Monte Albán, the
Zapotec capital, and Mitla, which
flourished above all during the Post-
Classic Period. El Tajín, in the
Veracruz region, was initially perhaps
a Totonac center and was later taken
over by the Huaxtecs. This is an
obligatory destination for a number
of reasons but primarily for its
connections with the ritual ball game.
In no other place have so many ball
courts been found or so many remains
connected with the sport.

Teotihuacan, the "City of the Gods,"
with its imposing pyramids and
roads, was the largest Mesoamerican
city of the Classic Period. Perhaps a
great center of pilgrimage, its political
and cultural influence extended over
other areas of Mesoamerica. Still
today, however, the identity of its
builders remains a mystery.

After the city had been abandoned,
the cultural heritage of Teotihuacan
was taken up by the inhabitants of
Xochicalco and Tula. At Tula, from
AD 900, the Toltecs developed the
ancient cult of the Feathered Serpent,
superimposing it over the figure of
their own cultural hero Topiltzin who
became known as Topiltzin
Quetzalcoatl. Tula, the archaeological
remains of which seem very modest
compared with the fabulous
descriptions of this Toltec capital,
contains architectural features typical
of the Post-Classic Period: atlantean
statues, chacmools, and *tzompantli*,
expressions of a society dominated by
a warrior aristocracy and pervaded by
sacrificial rituals. Identical elements
can be found in the impressive center
of Chichén Itzá, which, more than any
other site demonstrates the blending
and coexistence of the ancient Maya
culture with new Toltec elements of
Mexican origin. Chichén Itzá and Tula
fell into decline around the 12th
century AD, at the same time as the
Aztec empire, the last great power of
Pre-Columbian Mexico, was growing.

Next we proceed toward Lake
Texcoco and the remains of the great
dual city of Tenochtitlan–Tlatelolco.
Today, only a few ruins testify to the
magnificence of the ancient capital of
Motecuhzoma II, conquered by
Hernán Cortés in 1521.

141 (far left) Two massive cylindrical columns topped with rectangular capitals dominate the main entrance of the Palace of Chacmultún, a Maya center in the Yucatán, an example of the sober elegance of the Puuc architectural style.

141 (left) A mask of the god Chac, with his long, curling nose, overlooks the main entrance of the Palace of Xlapak, a Puuc site in the Yucatán.

141

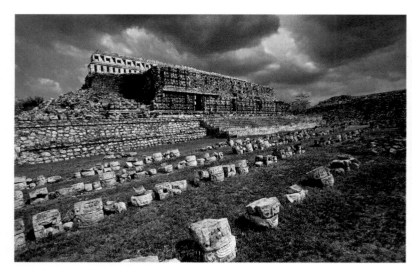

142 (opposite above left) Hundreds of large masks of the god Chac decorate the façades of the great Palace of the Masks at Kabah—hence its name.

142 (opposite above right) At Chicanná, a Yucatán site with Puuc-style architecture, the most celebrated structure is Building 2, the main entrance of which is formed by the open jaws of an earth monster.

142–143 (below left) The architecture of Edzná blends various styles which give this site particular charm. The "Five-Story Palace" seen here has a complex structure, unusual in a Maya architectural context.

143 (below) Stela H at Copán is one of a large number of such monuments that characterize this Maya city in Honduras. The rulers celebrated in this way are always depicted frontally and

with a solemn expression. This iconography is accompanied by cosmogonic and mythological symbols that lend the sculpture an almost baroque appearance.

144–145 (overleaf) An architectural detail from the Nunnery Quadrangle at Uxmal features a large mask representing the god Chac, with his gaping mouth and prominent nose.

The vast, and still partly unknown, Maya world demands its own self-contained itinerary. Many archaeological sites, rescued from the invading tropical vegetation, can still inspire the visitor today with a vision of the wealth enjoyed by these cities during the Classic Period. It has been established that the Maya, in contrast with the Aztecs, never created a true empire, rather series of confederations were created between various city states. The cities, while sharing common features, differed one from another and each had its own distinctive architectural elements and buildings. We begin with one of the richest and most prestigious cities, Palenque, which prospered under Pacal and his son Chan Bahlum.

We then continue through the Chiapas region toward the frontier between Mexico and Guatemala and reach Bonampak. Here the ruins preserve a cycle of exceptional wall paintings. We then visit three famous cities of the fertile Petén region; Yaxchilán, Uaxactún, and Tikal. After Teotihuacan, Tikal is one of the largest cities of Pre-Columbian Mesoamerica. Copán is the easternmost Mayan city, now in Honduras. Its ruined monuments never cease to surprise the visitor with their magnificence, originally intended to celebrate the glory of the ruling dynasty.

In the final centuries of the Classic Period, between AD 800 and 1000, the center of Maya culture shifted to the Yucatán, where cities such as Uxmal, Kabah, and Labná flourished under the influence of peoples arriving from Mexico, such as the Putún and the Chontál. These sites are interesting for their elegant Puuc-style architecture.

Once the Maya-Toltec cities of Chichén Itzá and Mayapán had declined, a number of fortified centers developed in the Yucatán region. Among these, Tulum, overlooking the Caribbean Sea, forms the final chapter in our archaeological itinerary. This was one of the last Maya strongholds of the Post-Classic Period up to 1518, when the Conquistadores landed on the coasts of Yucatán. Their captain, Juan de Grijalva, was captivated by the monuments of Tulum which he described as "more beautiful than Seville."

146–147 Located in a superb position on the Caribbean coast, the Maya city of Tulum has the appearance of a fortified citadel due not only to its walls, but also the severity of its architecture.

VILLAHERMOSA, HOME OF THE OLMEC COLOSSI

148 (below) This Colossal Head is somewhat different from the others as the facial features are only barely sketched in and a series of incisions seem to represent facial scarification.

149 (opposite) The Olmec Colossal Heads of La Venta weigh several tons and are still something of an enigma. Analysis indicates that the volcanic rock from which they are carved comes from the Tuxtla Mountains.

148 Some of the most impressive Olmec stone monuments are now to be found at the Villahermosa archaeological park. This is an altar, or throne, with a carving of a figure holding a child in its arms.

148 (bottom) Unique to the Olmec civilization are the Colossal Heads in volcanic stone, such as the one seen here. They may be portraits of high-ranking figures—perhaps warriors or kings.

In the Preclassic Period three principal centers of the Olmec civilization, San Lorenzo, La Venta, and Laguna de Los Cerros, were founded and began to develop in the tropical lowlands of the Gulf Coast region. Following the sudden and mysterious destruction of San Lorenzo, La Venta probably reached its cultural peak from around 900 BC. La Venta was built on an island in the midst of a swamp near the Tonalá river, on the eastern edge of the Olmec cultural area. Communities of farmers, artisans, and fishermen probably lived on the banks of the river not far from the island. The city covered an area of over 5 sq. km (2 sq. miles) and was a political and religious center of considerable importance between 900 and 400 BC.

The buildings of La Venta are aligned on a north–south axis and display a number of architectural and stylistic innovations that were unknown at San Lorenzo. These include three sophisticated serpentine mosaic floors that some scholars suggest depict jaguar masks. The site's most impressive monument is an imposing conical structure, 34 m (111 ft) high, made of beaten earth and located in the extreme south of the city. Its unique fluted form has been interpreted as symbolizing a volcano, perhaps one of the many in the Tuxtla region, the probable Olmec homeland.

The museum-park of Villahermosa in the modern state of Tabasco contains many of the stone monuments that are symbols of the Olmec culture: carved stelae, so-called "altars," which are more probably thrones, and the Colossal Heads with distinctive facial features, perhaps portraits of rulers. The volcanic stone for these monoliths was transported a considerable distance by river from the Tuxtla region.

The details of Olmec religion are still largely unknown, but one important aspect was handed down to successive cultures: the cult of the jaguar. It is impossible to discuss Olmec archaeology without examining this aspect, which is also a fundamental component of the history of Pre-Columbian Mesoamerica. In the iconography of the oldest civilizations in Mesoamerica, as well as areas of South America such as Peru, we find the constant presence of representations of an animal being with feline traits. In the Mesoamerican area this is referred to as the cult of the jaguar. The jaguar (*Panthera onca*) lives in the hot and humid tropical forests. Parts of Mexico, Guatemala, Belize, and the Amazon basin have always provided the ideal habitat for this animal. It is unknown in the Andes, but another big cat is found there, the puma (*Felis concolor*), whose name derives from a Quechua word, the language spoken by the Incas.

150 (opposite above left) The so-called altars from La Venta were more probably thrones. Their relief and three-dimensional decoration is linked to human or jaguar iconography. This is a hybrid being in a crouching position.

150 (opposite above right) This large Olmec sculpture in volcanic stone represents a seated figure wearing a headdress, with its legs crossed and arms resting on the knees in a solemn position of meditation.

The oldest images of the jaguar date back to the Olmecs, considered the "Mother Culture" of Mesoamerican civilization. Archaeology provides our only information about the Olmec pantheon and the evidence suggests that the Olmecs venerated a hybrid divinity born from the union between a human and a feline and depicted as a "were-jaguar." These images recur in the reliefs that decorate the stone monuments, frequently in association with other deities in animal form, such as birds, lizards, and snakes.

The Olmec heritage, including the jaguar cult, was handed down to the Mesoamerican cultures which followed over the centuries. These cultures depicted the jaguar deity with their own variations. Its presence is perhaps most prominent in the Maya pantheon, where it played a fundamental role, but it is also found at Veracruz, Teotihuacan, Monte Albán, and among peoples of the peripheral areas. In the Post-Classic Period the cult was also assimilated by the Toltecs and the Aztecs.

We must therefore ask why this particular animal deity was of such importance, and what were the reasons for its diffusion? As already discussed, Mesoamerican religion was based on "nahualism" and shamanic ritual. The word *Nahual* is an Aztec term meaning "disguise," and the Mayan form was *Uay*, which translates as "animal friend."

In the religious beliefs of the Zapotecs and the Maya, members of the elite and shamans were considered akin to divine beings and had a kind of alter-ego in the animal kingdom. By taking on the appearance of these animals they could enter into communication with the gods and the supernatural world. Shamans, who still exist in present-day Central America, can be considered as a sort of priest combined with a witch-doctor. Rather than communicating with the gods through simple offerings and prayer, they performed special hallucinatory rituals. Following prescribed dances, the letting of blood, and the taking of drugs, the shamans would enter into a state of trance and take on the

150–151 (below left) A huge altar, or throne, from La Venta features a niche from which emerges a seated figure with crossed legs, perhaps a shaman or a king. The decoration incised in the slab above the statue resembles the jaws of a jaguar.

151 (below) A number of mosaics at La Venta, such as the one seen here, have been been interpreted as representing the stylized mask of a jaguar.

appearance of their *Uay*, the animal alter-ego that would bring them into direct contact with a particular deity and allow them to experience supernatural visions. For the Olmecs and the Maya, the jaguar was considered the most important animal alter-ego, as indicated by the many images depicting kings and shamans together with jaguar-like beings.

Moreover, the jaguar was also regarded as embodying the nocturnal aspect of the sun god and was thus linked to the cult of the night. In this manifestation it was the custodian of the depths of the earth and its agricultural riches, and the caverns, which were conceived of as the means of access to the Underworld.

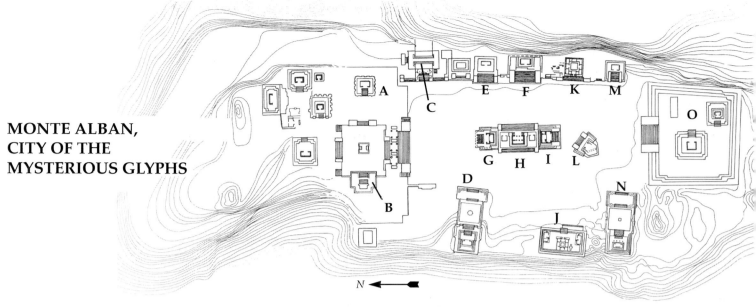

MONTE ALBAN, CITY OF THE MYSTERIOUS GLYPHS

The most important center in Oaxaca, Monte Albán, was founded at the end of the middle of Preclassic period, around 500 BC, by the Zapotecs. The peoples of the Oaxaca Valley had been in close contact with the Olmecs and they built on the foundations of the Olmec culture they had inherited. Archaeological research indicates that by as early as the middle of the Preclassic Period the Zapotecs of the Oaxaca region had "invented" writing and calendric calculations, and were responsible for their diffusion among other peoples. Traces of the oldest Mesoamerican calendar, the 260-day ritual calendar, have been found at Monte Albán.

A North Platform
B Building B
C Ball Court
D System IV
E Building U
F Building P
G Building G
H Building H
I Building I
J Temple of
   the Danzantes
K Building S or
   "The Palace"
L Building J or
   "The Observatory"
M Building Q
N System M
O South Platform

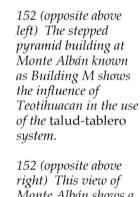

152 (opposite above left) The stepped pyramid building at Monte Albán known as Building M shows the influence of Teotihuacan in the use of the talud-tablero system.

152 (opposite above right) This view of Monte Albán shows a corner of the huge Main Plaza, along with Building M and the Temple of the Danzantes.

152–153 From the Preclassic Period to the late Classic, Monte Albán, in the Oaxaca region, was the "capital" of the Zapotec peoples. This panoramic view shows the Main Plaza, from Platform N.

153 (above) The North Platform, a detail of which is shown here, is the most imposing structure in Monte Albán. The complex borders the main plaza to the north and acts as a dividing element between the temple area and the city's residential zone.

153 (left) The cult of the jaguar and its related iconography have been found at Monte Albán, as shown by this terra-cotta statuette of a seated jaguar with a kind of "collar" or "scarf" around its neck.

These symbols date to the middle to late Preclassic Period and accompany an inscription on stone that has yet to be deciphered. There is some evidence for the use of writing and the development of the calendar in the Olmec world, from which the Zapotecs might have derived their knowledge. However, the evidence is scant and inconclusive.

Zapotec astronomical studies were closely linked with the calculation of time. Around 200 BC one of the most unusual buildings at Monte Albán, called Building J by archaeologists, was erected at the center of the Main Plaza. In plan this building has the shape of an arrow-head and was precisely aligned with the bright star Capella, from the point on the horizon where it rises to its zenith.

Monte Albán occupies high ground overlooking the Oaxaca Valley. Its earliest phase, known as Monte Albán I, dates back to a period between 500 and 100 BC and already features a series of stone-built structures. From this early phase the city developed into the most important religious and political center of Oaxaca over the course of just a few centuries.

Between 100 BC and AD 250 (Monte Albán II phase) the original nucleus of Monte Albán was transformed into an extensive and complex urban center with residential quarters that grew up in small compounds on artificial terraces carved into the hillside.

At the heart of the city was a great rectangular plaza around which numerous temple platforms (reached via broad stairways) and other ceremonial buildings were constructed in various phases. As in every other important Mesoamerican site, here too an area has been found that was laid out as a court for the ritual ball game. Conforming to the classic capital "I" shape, the Monte Albán ball court is distinguished by a series of niches, probably designed to hold images of the gods.

Building J was constructed at the center of the Main Plaza during the Monte Albán II phase. Another, earlier structure, however, is probably the best known and perhaps most representative of the Zapotec culture. This is the so-called Temple of the Danzantes, located on the west side of the plaza, in a central position between two structures that are similar to one another and date to a period between 400 and 200 BC.

Around the outside of this platform and on the steps of the external staircase is a series stone slabs,

154–155 (above) Most of the surviving monuments at Monte Albán date to the Classic Period occupation of the site. In the center of the Main Plaza is Building H, in front of which is Building J.

154 (opposite below left) Building J at Monte Albán, with its very unusual arrow-head shape pointing south-west, was probably used as an astronomical observatory. The Zapotecs possessed a high level of scientific and astronomical knowledge, which was inherited by the Maya.

154 (opposite below right) Building J at Monte Albán was aligned with the movements of the bright star Capella. Other Mesoamerican buildings, such as the Caracol at Chichén Itzá and the Tower of Palenque, may also have been used for astronomical observations.

155 (above) This detail of Building J shows a number of glyphs inscribed on one wall. They were originally painted and traces of color are still visible. The Zapotec writing system is the oldest known so far in Mesoamerica.

MITLA, PALACES
OF THE STONE MOSAICS

Following the decline and abandonment of Monte Albán, new Zapotec centers grew up, though on a smaller scale, including that at Mitla. This was a time of great upheavals elsewhere also, with many cities left in ruins. In the Post-Classic Period a new society appears dominated above all by a warrior caste, and an increased warlike outlook seems to have been the order of the day.

Five groups of buildings have been identified at Mitla that are considered as "palaces" and were built at ground level and on platforms. Internally the buildings are subdivided into long, narrow rooms, originally covered with flat roofs and arranged around huge courtyards.

One decorative innovation found here consists of attractive mosaics composed of small, finely cut stones set without mortar to form geometric and serpentine motifs in friezes along the external walls. The so-called Group of the Columns consisting of the structures known as the "North Court" and "South Court," represents the largest and most elegantly proportioned architectural complex in Mitla.

The North Court is surrounded on three sides by long halls each with three entrances; the external corners of these buildings do not touch one another. Through the "Hall of Columns" which takes its name from the six monolithic columns that supported the roof, is a small and completely enclosed courtyard onto which face the four rooms. These were the apartments in which the most important priest of the city lived. The Hall of Columns is rightly considered to be the most attractive of Mitla's monuments. Its architecture recalls that of the Palace of the Governor at Uxmal, datable to the same period.

164–165 (left) Mitla replaced Monte Albán as the dominant center of the Oaxaca region. One of Mitla's most prestigious buildings, the Hall of the Columns, retains traces of color and the magnificent stone mosaic frieze on its façade.

164 (opposite below left) Archaeological research at Mitla has revealed the presence of important tombs with complex architectural structures, such as Tomb 1 shown here. Unfortunately, the tombs had lost all their original contents.

164 (opposite below right) The Hall of Columns owes its name to the monolithic pillars that once supported its flat roof. It is a good example of the graceful architecture of Mitla.

165 (top) The architecture of Mitla is much admired for its elegance and the originality of its mosaics of perfectly cut stone. This room in the Hall of the Columns is called the Room of the Friezes after the mosaic decoration on the walls.

165 (bottom) A unique feature of the buildings at Mitla are the attractive mosaics that decorate the walls, forming geometric and serpentine motifs such as this one from the Hall of the Columns. Some of the friezes recall the Puuc style of the cities of the Yucatán of the same period.

As at Monte Albán, tombs have been discovered at Mitla, although fewer in number, that were reused up to the Spanish Conquest. The complex structure of these tombs, often cruciform in plan, means that they resemble underground houses and were even decorated in a similar fashion, with stone mosaics and frescoes. Unfortunately, we have no information about the funerary treasure buried with the dead due to this practice of reusing the tombs, which has meant that over the centuries their contents have been lost. They may have been similar to the treasures of the same period found in the Mixtec tombs of Monte Albán.

166 Long friezes with geometric motifs made of stone mosaics are still miraculously preserved on one of the exterior walls of the Hall of the Columns.

166 The Hall of the Columns, like many other residential buildings at Mitla, has an elongated rectangular plan and is sited on a low platform.

The Mixtecs, the "People of the Clouds," who took over most of the territory of the Zapotecs, have left a series of documents—beautiful codices written not on bark fiber like those of the Maya, but on deer skins. One has been identified as a religious-mythological text while the others deal with historical themes concerning the dynastic succession of their rulers.

Because the Mixtec writing system is essentially pictographic it is difficult to decipher: only the signs for the names of figures and calendric symbols indicating the dates of birth of kings, based on the 260-day Ritual Calendar, have been deciphered with any certainty.

Pictorial images, painted in bright colors, prevail over glyphs which perhaps are more simple than those of Zapotecs and the Maya but are pictographic, phonetic, or even mixed. The tradition of pictographic codices was probably passed on by the Mixtecs to the Aztecs.

166–167 (above) and 167 (right) It is thought that the elegant palaces of Mitla, with their façades covered with refined geometric motifs, were the residences or administrative centers of a powerful priestly caste, perhaps led by a "High Priest."

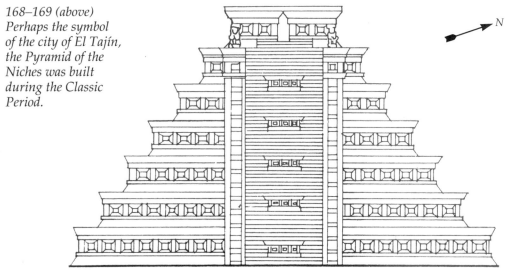

168–169 (above) Perhaps the symbol of the city of El Tajín, the Pyramid of the Niches was built during the Classic Period.

N

EL TAJIN, AN ARCHITECTURE OF LIGHT AND SHADOW

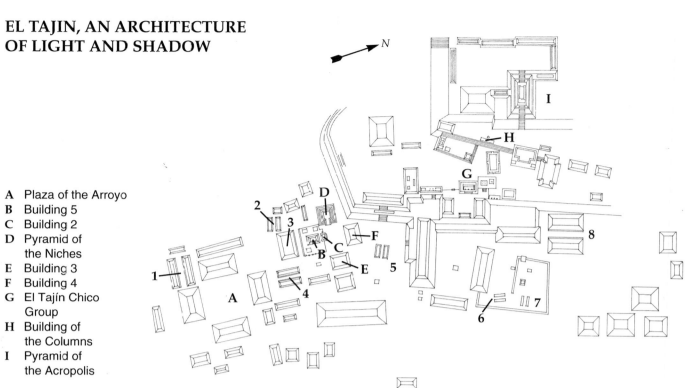

A   Plaza of the Arroyo
B   Building 5
C   Building 2
D   Pyramid of
    the Niches
E   Building 3
F   Building 4
G   El Tajín Chico
    Group
H   Building of
    the Columns
I   Pyramid of
    the Acropolis

1–8 Ball courts

168 (opposite below) The plan and elevation of the great Pyramid of the Niches at El Tajín reveal that the structure had a square base and consisted of six tiers. Its architectural form and elements show clear influences from Teotihuacan, for instance the use of the talud-tablero *system, but the temple's distinctive feature is the series of 365 niches creating a play of light and shadow.*

169 (above) The ceremonial center of El Tajín features pyramids of modest size in which the Teotihuacan model has been adapted to the regional style of the Gulf Coast. In this view Building 16 is visible on the right and the Pyramid of the Niches on the left.

Around AD 250 a civilization with a wealth of unusual features flourished in the coastal region of Veracruz, hence the name often given it, Classic Veracruz. Its founders have not been identified with certainty, though some think they were the Totonacs. El Tajín was its principal site, named after a Totonac god of thunder, rain, and fertility.

In this major ceremonial center, the important role of the calculation of time is reflected in the architecture. Its most impressive temple is the Pyramid of the Niches. This imposing,

though not very large, building consists of six superimposed levels, the external façades of which are decorated with 365 niches, presumably relating to the number of days in the solar year. It seems probable, therefore, that the pyramid was in some way linked to astronomy, as were structures at Uaxactún, Uxmal, and elsewhere.

The interiors of the niches were originally painted dark red, while the borders were turquoise, creating dazzling effects in the bright light. Archaeological research has now

169

170 (opposite above left) A panel relief decorating a ball court building at El Tajín. One of the figures has clear rabbit attributes.

170 (opposite above right) The large ceremonial center of El Tajín includes numerous buildings and ball courts. This view shows so-called

Building C, the structure of which is composed of three superimposed volumes. Long friezes with a fret motif decorate the walls.

shown that all the other buildings of the city were also finished with polychrome stucco.

El Tajín, like Monte Albán, extends over a vast area; however, in contrast with the latter, the religious and civic buildings are randomly distributed on artificial platforms set around numerous squares. The *talud-tablero* element, inherited from Teotihuacan, was adapted to local styles and enriched with original decorative motifs giving the buildings a very exuberant appearance.

El Tajín is mostly renowned, however, for the number of its ball courts, which were built throughout the Classic Period. As discussed earlier, evidence for the ritual ball game is found as early as the Olmec era in the fertile regions of the Gulf Coast where rubber was produced in abundance. The great number of ball courts found in El Tajín has prompted suggestions that the city hosted annual ball game championships, comparable in importance with the Olympic Games of ancient Greece. Representatives from neighboring regions and perhaps even further afield might have thronged to the city to participate in these championships, possibly linked to particular religious cults and festivals.

Objects related to the ritual ball game made by the people of El Tajín were exported widely. They consist of stone replicas of objects used by the players during the games, today known as "yokes," "*palmas*," and "*hachas*." "Yokes," generally horseshoe-shaped, were originally made of padded leather and were worn as protective belts; the "*palmas*" acted as breastplates while the "*hachas*" were perhaps score markers. These stone objects were carved with complex relief decorations in the form

of intertwined volutes, spirals, and plant and animal motifs. They were undoubtedly made for ritual use and have mainly been found in tombs.

Another characteristic Classic Veracruz craft product are the so-called "smiling statuettes." These are attractive clay figurines, skillfully made with careful attention to detail. Their smiling, almost laughing expressions have been interpreted as depicting participants in rituals in which worshipers reached states of ecstasy.

170–171 (left) El Tajín's monuments do not have such imposing dimensions as those of Teotihuacan or many Maya cities of the Classic Period. In the foreground left stands Building 16, behind which is the Pyramid of the Niches. The use of niches associated with the talud-tablero *system to create a play of light and shade is a particular feature of the architecture of Veracruz.*

171 (above) Building 16 also features the use of niches typical of El Tajín, creating interesting patterns of horizontals and verticals.

172 (right) This view shows just one part of the extensive site of Teotihuacan. In the background, at the end of the long, straight Avenue of the Dead, rises the majestic Pyramid of the Moon, flanked by minor buildings.

172–173 (below) A view of Teotihuacan from the top of the Pyramid of the Moon. On the left, next to the Avenue of the Dead, is the imposing Pyramid of the Sun.

TEOTIHUACAN, THE CITY OF THE GODS

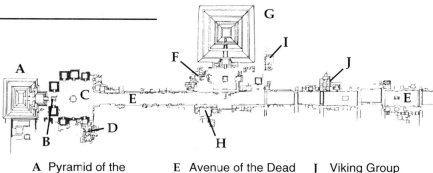

A Pyramid of the Moon
B Building of the Altars
C Plaza of the Moon
D Palace of Quetzalpapalotl
E Avenue of the Dead
F Palace of the Sun
G Pyramid of the Sun
H Patio of the Four Temples
I House of the Priests
J Viking Group
K The Citadel
L Temple of the Quetzalcoatl
M Gran Conjunto

Not far from Mexico City lie the remains of the ancient city of Teotihuacan, the "City of the Gods." Many Mexican myths of Pre-Columbian origin speak of Teotihuacan, alluding to it as a special, magical city. According to one of these myths, it was the place of creation of the sun of the Fifth Era, in which the Mexican people thought of themselves as living prior to the arrival of the Spanish Conquistadores.

In contrast with many cities buried under volcanic ash or destroyed by war and long forgotten, Teotihuacan continued to live on in the memories

of the Mesoamerican peoples even after its decline. Still today historians and archaeologists are investigating the reasons for the long cultural shadow cast by this site, just as they are exploring the meaning of the city's great pyramids.

Other sites flourished during the Preclassic Period before the rise of Teotihuacan, including Cuicuilco, Tlatilco, and Tlapacoya. The first was destroyed by the violent eruption of the volcano Xitle around 200 BC; remains of the buildings buried by the ash have been uncovered, including a large circular platform, demonstrating the importance of the site. It is presumed that the survivors from Cuicuilco took refuge at Teotihuacan, bringing with them the cult of the god of fire and new life to the primitive settlement. The oldest traces of a Preclassic village in the Teotihuacan area date back to 500 BC, corresponding to the pre-urban phase in the city's development.

Around 100 BC, following the influx of immigrants from Cuicuilco, a true ceremonial center began to take shape and the oldest sacred buildings

173 (above) Numerous masks have been found at Teotihuacan, which are among the finest in the whole of Mesoamerica. The city's craftsmen excelled in the working of stone, jade, and terra-cotta. This beautiful example is carved from stone; the sunken bands would originally have been inlaid.

173 (left) This terra-cotta figurine from Teotihuacan represents the god known as Xipe-Totec, "Our Lord the Flayed One," to the Aztecs, who still worshiped him in the era of the Spanish Conquest.

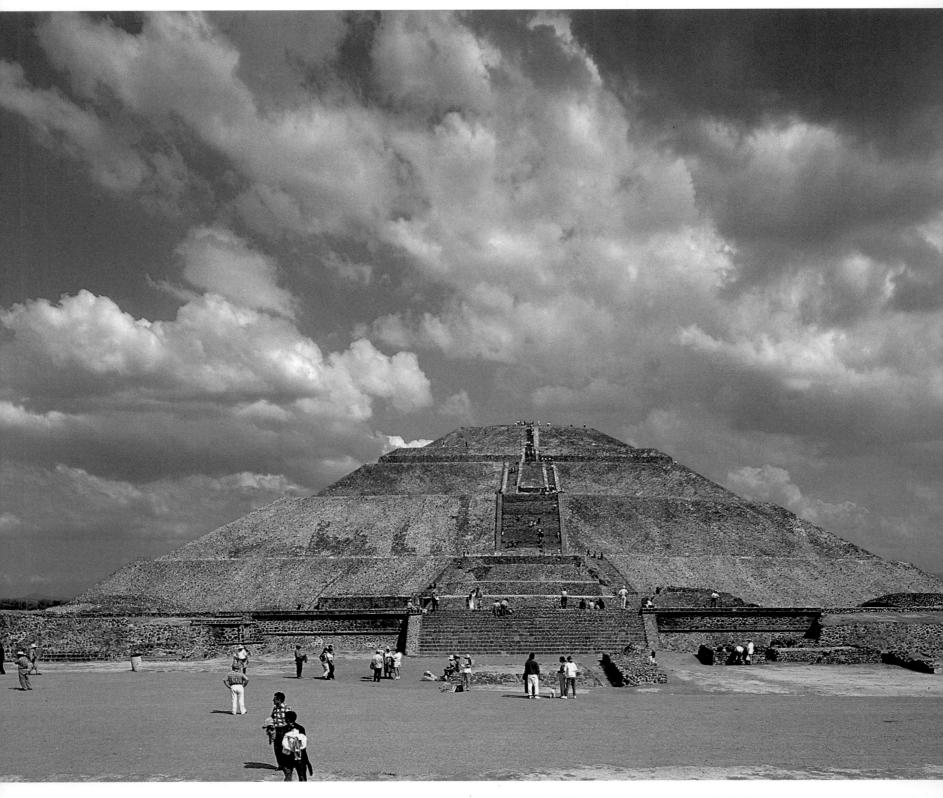

174–175 (above) An impression of the size and power of the Pyramid of the Sun at Teotihuacan is conveyed by this view. A stairway narrowing toward the top leads to the summit, 65 m (213 ft) high. Originally the pyramid would have been even taller, due to the sanctuary on the summit which has now disappeared.

174 (right) An aerial view of the Pyramid of the Sun at Teotihuacan reveals a simple yet majestic stepped pyramid.

175 (top) This profile clearly shows the talud-tablero system which is a hallmark of Teotihuacan architecture and was subsequently adopted by many of the peoples of Mesoamerica.

175 (center) This platform next to the Pyramid of the Sun is considered by some scholars to be the remains of an ancient residential building, known as the Palace of the Sun.

175 (bottom) The Pyramid of the Sun, overlooking the Plaza of the Sun, rises above the other religious complexes of Teotihuacan stretched out along the Avenue of the Dead.

perhaps date from this period. During the 1st century AD the so-called Avenue of the Dead was laid out and the two temples, the great Pyramid of the Sun and, slightly later, the Pyramid of the Moon, were built along it. Below the Pyramid of the Sun archaeologists have discovered a cave in the form of a long tunnel, which perhaps explains the choice of this particular site for the massive temple.

The Pyramid of the Sun is the largest building in Teotihuacan and the second largest in Mesoamerica after the great pyramid of Cholula. Today it reaches a height of 65 m (213 ft), but it was once even higher as it was originally crowned by a sanctuary, probably built of perishable materials. The main body of the pyramid is composed of adobe bricks and rubble, finished with stucco. Below its base, the tunnel-like cave was probably a natural feature, modified and enlarged by man, probably beginning in the Preclassic Period. It is subdivided into small rooms and had a religious function. It has been suggested that there may be a link between this ancient grotto and the legendary place of origin of the Aztecs called Chicomotzóc which translates as "The Place of the Seven Caverns," although no evidence exists for a common origin for the two civilizations.

One particularly interesting aspect of the Pyramid of the Sun is the fact that it is oriented to the passage of the sun from dawn to dusk and the point on the horizon at which the Pleiades rise at the equinoxes. Most probably, therefore, the name of the temple, as told to the Spanish by the Aztecs, is in reality much older.

176 (right) Running north to south through Teotihuacan, the Avenue of the Dead is around 4 km (2½ miles) long. At its northern end rises the Pyramid of the Moon.

176–177 (below) The Pyramid of the Moon rises to a height of 46 m (151 ft), dominating the square of the same name. Like the Pyramid of the Sun it is composed of five levels.

The Pyramid of the Moon, again an Aztec name, was built slightly later and is also slightly smaller than the Pyramid of the Sun. Located at the northern end of the Avenue of the Dead, it consists of five superimposed tiers and it too conceals a series of rooms that were places of worship.

On the western side of the Plaza of the Moon are a number of important buildings, including the Palace of Quetzalpapalotl. Its structure and elaborate style of architecture suggest that this may have been the residence of individuals belonging to the city's ruling caste—possibly members of the priesthood and at the same time heads of a mercantile corporation. Here can be found some of the best examples of the wall paintings of Teotihuacan, in which shades of red predominate.

Inside the palace are a number of patios; the principal one is surrounded by four small rooms, three of which still retain their central roof support. These columns are decorated with magnificent reliefs depicting a mythical being, the Quetzal Butterfly—hence the name of the building—surrounded by other symbolic elements linked to the cult of water. Quetzalpapalotl is a Nahuatl word and we know that the Aztecs worshiped a female divinity of this name. Depictions of the goddess at Teotihuacan suggest an ancient origin for this cult, which was still practiced in the Post-Classic Period.

At the threshold of the 2nd century AD Teotihuacan began to expand and was enriched by new buildings along the north–south axis of the Avenue of the Dead and the east–west axis of a second avenue. The intersection of the two divided the city into four sections, where the palaces of the elite were surrounded by the homes of ordinary people. Around AD 200, the Pyramid of Quetzalcoatl, one of the most emblematic monuments of the city, was erected within the so-called citadel or Ciudadela.

Teotihuacan reached its peak in the middle of the Classic Period, between AD 250 and 650. In this period it had all the hallmarks of a great metropolis, extended over an area of 22 sq. km (8½ sq. miles), and had a population of between 75,000 and 200,000.

177 (below) Two views of some of the eleven minor temples located around the Plaza of the Moon, which was once the setting for important ceremonies.

A large number of residential quarters, consisting of buildings with complex structures, courtyards, cisterns, sewers, and roads flanked by canals, developed alongside the imposing ceremonial complexes and the residences of the ruling caste. Teotihuacan was laid out in a very regular fashion, with careful planning and a grid system based on a unit of 57 sq. m (614 sq. ft). Even the small river that flowed through the city was diverted to conform to the grid layout. Typical architectural features were precise alignment, symmetry, and the use of simple columns.

So who were the ingenious people who constructed such a vast and "modern" metropolis, the economic, religious, and cultural influence of which extended far and wide? Glyphs found in the wall paintings are not yet fully understood and thus cannot help answer this question. The identity of the people of Teotihuacan is therefore still not known for certain.

It is presumed that the population was composed of craftsmen, farmers, and merchants who were governed by a powerful priesthood devoted the cult of a Great Goddess. Many of the wall paintings decorating the palaces depict scenes linked to fertility and agriculture. One of the most celebrated is known as the "Paradise of the Rain God," or "Tlalocan," but is now interpreted as depicting a strange spider goddess. Another cult was that of the Feathered Serpent, as illustrated by the sculptures decorating the great Pyramid of Quetzalcoatl.

The sophisticated craft products of Teotihuacan were exported throughout Mesoamerica: vessels and masks in stone and pottery, textiles, and jewelry of precious stones. Other aspects of Teotihuacan culture were also spread far afield, such as the so-called *talud-tablero* system used in temple architecture. Similar architectural features were also adopted by the Maya and Maya-Toltec peoples in the great centers of the Yucatán in the Post-Classic Period.

Perhaps around AD 650, or possibly a century earlier, this greatest metropolis of central Mexico was burned and destroyed. The causes are unknown—perhaps it was an invasion by unknown peoples, or internal strife. Many inhabitants sought refuge in the nearby center of Azapozalco which had for some time been in Teotihuacan's cultural orbit.

178 (top) A detail of a carved wall relief from the Temple of Quetzalcoatl showing a shell and two sea-snails below the sinuous, feathered body of the serpent. Such iconography suggests a link between this cult and that of water.

178 (above) A great stairway of dizzying steepness leads in a single flight to the top of the Pyramid of Quetzalcoatl. It is flanked by sloping surfaces decorated with serpents' heads, a symbol of the deity, carved in the round on every tablero.

178–179 (right) This extraordinary sculpture is one of the Feathered Serpent heads decorating a façade of the Pyramid of Quetzalcoatl. The feline features are accentuated by the teeth exposed in the gaping jaws. Strangely, the head, carved in the round, appears to emerge from a flower. It is joined to the sinuous body of the Feathered Serpent depicted in low relief on the wall. The presence of this iconography on a building in Teotihuacan dating from the early Classic Period suggests that the cult of Quetzalcoatl had very ancient origins.

180–181 Bright colors enlivened the magnificent Pyramid of Quetzalcoatl, which rose in the center of the so-called Citadel or Ciudadela of Teotihuacan. On each tier was carved the undulating body of the feathered serpent, while between, the head of the god alternated with that of a mysterious divinity, perhaps identifiable as Tlaloc.

According to scholars, people of Toltec origin arriving from the north subsequently took over the city, fusing its culture with the religious beliefs that they brought with them. What is certain is that by around AD 900 Teotihuacan had been definitively abandoned. When, five centuries later, the Aztecs arrived in the city they were stunned by the immense ruins and, unable to believe that such structures were the work of man, it was they who named it the "City of the Gods."

Available archaeological evidence is unable to resolve the problem of the abandonment of the powerful metropolis that for centuries had dominated the Mexican valleys. Certain factors suggest that the founders of Tula were the inhabitants of Teotihuacan, combined with the Toltec invaders to whom they passed on the cult of the Feathered Serpent.

182 (opposite below right) This is a detail of one of the most unusual and elegant structures of Teotihuacan: the Patio of the Columns in the Palace of Quetzalpapalotl which in Nahuatl means "Quetzal Butterfly." The massive pillars that support the roof of the rooms facing onto the courtyard retain traces of their original polychrome decoration.

183 (below center) Beautiful frescoes decorate the rooms in the building known as the Temple of Mythological Animals. The one shown here depicts a feline with a feathered headdress.

183 (bottom) This terra-cotta almena— an architectural element that probably sat on the roof of a building in Teotihuacan— represents a bird from whose beak emerges a speech scroll.

182–183 (above) The massive pillars of the Patio of the Columns, the elegant courtyard within the Palace of Quetzalpapalotl, were carved with relief decorations. This stylized image of a bird, probably the "Quetzal Butterfly" after which the building is named, is set in a frame of geometric motifs, perhaps glyphs.

182 (opposite below left) Given its position in the southwestern corner of the Plaza of the Moon, it is thought that the Palace of Quetzalpapalotl, of which a section is seen here, was the sumptuous residence of a powerful priest.

TULA, LEGENDARY CAPITAL OF THE TOLTECS

A Ball court
B Adoratorio or central altar
C Pyramid C
D Palacio Quemado, "palace"
E Pyramid B
F Burned Palace
G Ball court

184 (below) "Atlanteans" are a very characteristic form of Toltec art. These are statues of male figures with military attributes that were used as supports for roofs. This smaller version, made of basalt, is 73 cm (29 in) tall, and would have supported a slab of stone for either an altar or a throne.

Today, the site of Tula in the modern state of Hidalgo appears to visitors to be a modest center compared with ancient descriptions of the prestigious capital of the Toltec civilization. According to traditional accounts, the city was founded in AD 968, when the leader Ce Acatl Topiltzin, later known as Quetzalcoatl, created a new capital to replace the ancient Colhuacan.

The subsequent colonization of Chichén Itzá by the Toltecs under the leadership of Quetzalcoatl perhaps explains the strong stylistic and architectural similarities between the two sites. However, one curious fact is that the "colonized" center today appears to be much wealthier and larger than the "colonizing" city.

At Tula, architectural elements that originated in Teotihuacan, such as the *talud-tablero* system, are found mixed with innovative elements that reveal Toltec influence, often military in

nature and linked to bloodthirsty rituals. The very position of the city, on a promontory, must have been chosen with defense in mind.

Among the characteristic elements of the site are the chacmools, stone figures of reclining males. In the popular imagination these are believed to be altars for human hearts, but it is now thought that they were used for various offerings. Another feature is the *tzompantli*, a copy in stone of a rack on which skulls were displayed, testimony, perhaps, of an intensification of the practice of human sacrifice.

The most impressive building in Tula, located on the central plaza, is Pyramid B, in front of which are the remains of a great pillared hall. Crowning the pyramid platform are the monolithic statues known as atlanteans, which probably acted as supporting columns for the roof of an outer room of the temple. Depicting Toltec warriors, their severe and rigid expressions must have awed visitors. On their heads they wear crowns of feathers and a headband with ear-flaps. On their chests are eagle or butterfly motifs in relief.

At the base of Pyramid B are the majestic surviving colonnades of the so-called "Burned Palace" which owes its name to the discovery during archaeological excavations of the remains of the roof beams, destroyed in a fire in AD 1168.

184–185 On the summit of the platform of Pyramid B are gigantic basalt statues and various pillars, carved with relief motifs, that originally supported the roof of the temple.

The statues, known as "atlanteans," almost certainly depict Toltec warriors. These impressive sculptures still retain traces of the colors with which they were originally decorated.

184 (opposite below) At the foot of Pyramid B are the ruins of the colonnade forming part of the so-called Burned Palace, destroyed by fire in around AD 1168.

185 (above right) Much of Toltec art has a military aspect: this polychrome relief in stone represents two warriors with shields and crests.

186 (right) One of the figures immortalized in the frieze decorating the Temple of the Feathered Serpent at Xochicalco: he is seated under a sinuous curve of the body of the Feathered Serpent that runs along the frieze.

186–187 (below) The magnificent Temple of the Feathered Serpent has a unique profile in Mesoamerica architecture. It consists of one large talud-tablero element, with a particularly tall talud and a tablero crowned with a projecting cornice.

187 (opposite below left) A view of the cosmopolitan city of Xochicalco, which may have flourished with the decline of Teotihuacan.

187 (opposite right above) The Temple of the Feathered Serpent occupies a central position in Xochicalco's main square.

XOCHICALCO AND THE CALENDAR

187 (below right) The imposing ruins of Xochicalco extend over a series of low hills and the principal complex, shown here, takes the form of a vast terraced acropolis.

A Seashells, symbol of the wind and the Feathered Serpent
B Calendric symbol
C Scales of the Feathered Serpent
D Feathered Serpent
E Calendric symbol

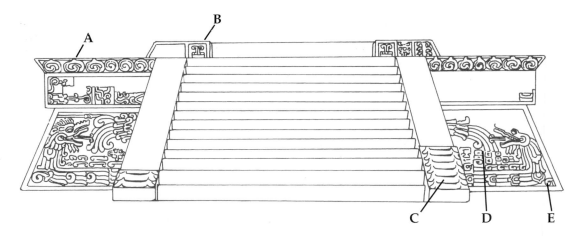

The city of Xochicalco, in the present-day Mexican state of Morelos, entered a period of great prosperity around AD 700. With the collapse of the political and economic hegemony of Teotihuacan, by which it had been overshadowed, Xochicalco became the principal trading center of the region. It was favorably sited on the trade route linking the Mexican plateau with the Balsas river that was used by merchants in cotton, cacao, precious stones, feathers, and obsidian.

Xochicalco's commercial and cultural contacts extended as far as Zapotec and Mixtec Oaxaca and Veracruz. It was thus a cosmopolitan city, and the inhabitants, with their widespread contacts combined with a probable legacy from Teotihuacan, successfully assumed a leading role in the region, from an intellectual and an economic point of view. This is revealed by the traces of a writing system and the use of calendric glyphs.

Xochicalco's ceremonial center, like that of Tula, was built on an elevated site and shows traces of fortification. The temples, porticoes, and ball court, which has striking similarities with that at Copán and is one of the oldest on the Mexican Plateau, are grouped around a principal plaza. There are many signs of strong Maya influence, as well as that of Teotihuacan, of which Xochicalco was probably never a "colony," but rather a rival city.

Certain monuments at Xochicalco were linked to calendric studies. The oldest and most widely used Mesoamerican calendar was the 260-day cycle or Ritual Calendar, known as *tzolkin* to the Maya and *tonalpohualli* to the Aztecs, which is thought of as a divinatory almanac.

It was composed of 20 named days and the figures from 1 to 13,

combinations of which could be favorable or unfavorable. The first day of the Maya calendar was 1 Imix: 260 days would pass before such a combination of number and name would reappear, a figure obtained by multiplying 20 by 13.

As well as the Ritual Calendar there was also the civic or solar calendar composed of 360 days plus 5, that is to say 18 months of 20 days each, to which was added a very short month of just five unnamed days which were considered to be unpropitious.

In order for the same date to coincide in the two different systems,

of which the civic calendar is by far the longer, 18,980 days had to pass, that is to say a cycle of 52 years. Maya texts of the Classic Period, which are found carved in stone or painted in the surviving codices, are narrations of historical events, accompanied by precise dates. These dates are based on yet another calendar, the so-called "Long Count."

The point of departure for the Long Count was a specific but mythological moment corresponding to 2 August, 3114 BC. This date can be considered as the Maya "Year Zero." The Long Count was subdivided into periods of

20 days, making it a vigesimal system, corresponding to the concept of the month, which was known as *uinal*; 18 uinals made up a *tun*, that is to say a year of 360 days. Twenty years formed a *katun* and 20 *katuns* equalled a *baktun*.

A simplified version, known as the Short Count, was devised from the Long Count in the Post-Classic Period. An important role was also played by calendars linked to the cycles of the moon, also known as the Supplementary Series, and those that related to the cycles of the planet Venus and the solar eclipses.

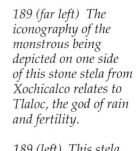

188–189 (left) A detail of the frieze decorating the external walls of the Temple of the Feathered Serpent at Xochicalco. The iconography is linked with the cult of the Feathered Serpent, here represented with gaping feline jaws, as also at the Pyramid of Quetzalcoatl at Teotihuacan. Calendric glyphs are incised on the wall.

189 (right) The funerary mask and jewelry seen here come from Xochicalco, but their style and craftsmanship show the clear influence of the culture of Teotihuacan.

189 (far left) The iconography of the monstrous being depicted on one side of this stone stela from Xochicalco relates to Tlaloc, the god of rain and fertility.

189 (left) This stela, like the previous example, is decorated with relief carving. The iconography is again religious and concerns the birth of the god Quetzalcoatl. In contrast with the frieze on the Temple of the Feathered serpent, however, the deity is here represented in his anthropomorphic form.

190 (right) A serpent head forms the base of one of the pillars at the top of the Temple of the Warriors at Chichén Itzá. The symbolism of the cult of the Feathered Serpent is found throughout the city.

190–191 A view of perhaps the two most prestigious buildings at Chichén Itzá, the Temple of the Warriors and the Court of the Thousand Columns, with the tropical forest in the background.

CHICHEN ITZA, JAGUARS AND FEATHERED SERPENTS

A "Nunnery"
   (Casa de las Monjas)
B Temple of the Wall
   Panels
C Caracol (Observatory)
D Red House
E Cenote Xtoloc
F High Priest's Tomb
G Mercado
H Hall of the
   Thousand Columns
I Temple of the
   Warriors
J "Castillo"
K Platform of the Cones
L Platform of the
   Eagles
M Tzompantli
N Great Ball Court
O Temple of the
   Jaguars
P Sacred Cenote

Chichén Itzá is a spectacular example of a what may be described as a Maya-Toltec city. Perhaps under the influence of "colonizers" from Tula, it flourished and reached a considerable size. The myths and traditions of the city, shrouded in legend, offer an intriguing framework for an examination of its architectural and stylistic aspects, characterized by the clear blending of two cultures.

Numerous decorative elements found at Chichén Itzá, especially stone sculptures and reliefs, attest to the importance of the cult of Quetzalcoatl. In the complex iconography and style of these sculptures we may perhaps be able to discern a meeting point between myth and archaeology. It was probably the Toltecs who superimposed their cultural hero Topiltzin Quetzalcoatl, the legendary king of the city of Tula (identified by archaeologists as the city in the modern state of Hidalgo), upon the ancient and mysterious deity represented as the Feathered Serpent. In Toltec mythology, after ruling the city of Tula for many years, Quetzalcoatl was dethroned by the evil Tezcatlipoca; according to the sources this took place in AD 987.

Two intertwined legends recount the destiny of this hero after his expulsion from Tula. According to one, he emigrated to the east with a group of followers, reaching the Yucatán region, probably by sea. This agrees with Yucatec documents from the Colonial era which tell of the arrival at Chichén Itzá of an educated and sophisticated figure of noble birth,

191 (center) At the base of the Temple of the Warriors at Chichén Itzá is a maze of pillars forming a portico. The square pillars are decorated with relief carvings depicting warriors in Toltec costumes, hence the name of the temple.

191 (bottom) Among the architectural elements introduced by the Toltecs are cylindrical pillars and columns forming colonnades, which are rare in other Mesoamerican sites of the Classic Period. This view shows the columns with rectangular capitals that supported the roof of the large hypostyle "Hall of the Thousand Columns."

whom the Maya called Kukulcan, which in the Yucatec language means "Serpent-Quetzal", or more simply "Feathered Serpent." He is said to have brought great knowledge to Chichén Itzá, especially in the fields of the arts and medicine, as well as the culture of his city of origin. It was this knowledge, assimilated by the local peoples, that provided the stimulus for the prosperity of Chichén Itzá and neighboring cities. Many historians have interpreted the oral traditions and Colonial sources as a "romantic" version of historical events: the "newcomers" to Chichén Itzá were probably exiles of Toltec stock, forced out of Tula by other peoples.

From the end of the 10th century AD Chichén Itzá assumed the role of the leading city in the Yucatán region. Its architecture represented a combination of elements inherited from the Maya of the Late Classic

192 (below center) A human figure, perhaps a priest, stands on the upper section of the Temple of the Warriors. Below him a snake's head carved in the round with gaping jaws forms a decorative element on the edge of the great central stairway.

192 (left below) This platform supported by smaller versions of the atlantean pillars known at Tula stands in the Temple of the Warriors at Chichén Itzá. It probably served as the throne of the ruler of the city, though some see it as a sacrificial altar.

192 (below) A tiny figure carved in the round as if emerging from the jaws of a monstrous bird of prey forms a decoration of a wall in the Temple of the Warriors.

192 (bottom) Another detail of the frieze decorating the Temple of the Warriors of Chichén Itzá which depicts a series of eagles and jaguars, a recurrent theme in the iconography of sculptures in Toltec ceremonial centers.

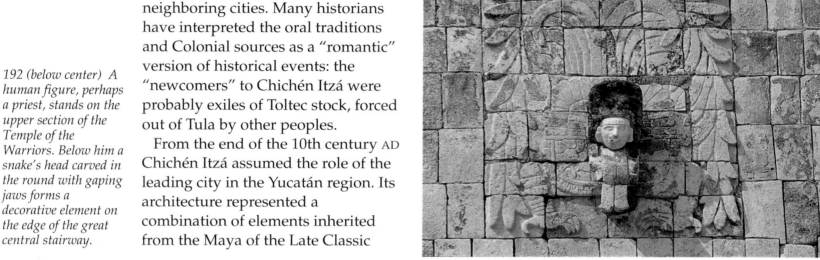

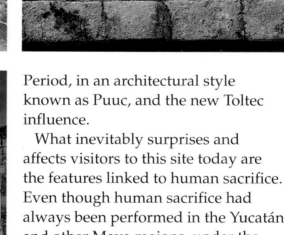

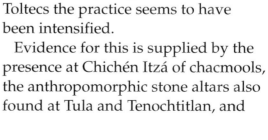

Period, in an architectural style known as Puuc, and the new Toltec influence.

What inevitably surprises and affects visitors to this site today are the features linked to human sacrifice. Even though human sacrifice had always been performed in the Yucatán and other Maya regions, under the Toltecs the practice seems to have been intensified.

Evidence for this is supplied by the presence at Chichén Itzá of chacmools, the anthropomorphic stone altars also found at Tula and Tenochtitlan, and

193 (opposite) The great Temple of the Warriors at Chichén Itzá represents a cultural hybrid of Maya and Toltec elements. On the top of the pyramid stands a chacmool, the anthropomorphic altar for offerings. In the background can be seen the columns and pillars that supported the roof of the temple.

the *tzompantli*, a copy in stone of the rack on which skulls of decapitated victims were displayed.

Another important feature at Chichén Itzá is the Sacred Cenote. This is a very deep well, into the dark and murky waters of which selected victims and a variety of rich offerings were thrown to placate the rain god Chac–Tlaloc. Such "sacred wells" are found not only at Chichén Itzá, but also at many other urban centers in the region. The term "cenote," adopted by the Spanish, derives from the Yucatec Maya word *dzonot* which was used for the natural circular wells formed in the landscape by the dissolution of limestone. In some cases, where the water table lies at great depths, the wells were only accessible via long ladders which the locals lowered through caves and tunnels in the rock. A famous example is the so-called "Cave of Bolonchén."

The primary function of the cenote was as a reservoir of fresh water and archaeologists have noted that around such wells there are usually also traces of human settlement dating back to the earliest periods. In many places, however, cenotes were also used for the sacrifice of humans and animals and they were thought of as a means of access to Xibalbá, the Maya kingdom of the Underworld. The Sacred Cenote at Chichén Itzá was still visited for ritual purposes even after the Spanish Conquest.

The sacred area of the city, linked to the Cenote by a long road, is

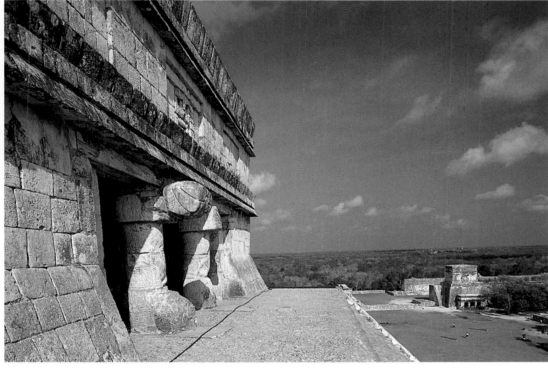

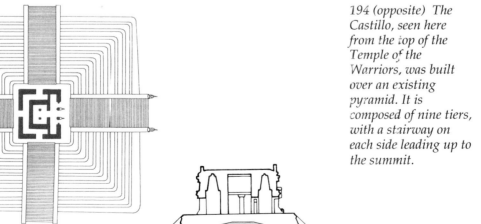

194 (opposite) The Castillo, seen here from the top of the Temple of the Warriors, was built over an existing pyramid. It is composed of nine tiers, with a stairway on each side leading up to the summit.

195 (left) A plan and elevation of the Castillo. The profile view reveals the existence of the earlier temple, completely incorporated within the more recent building.

195 (above left) A detail of the Castillo: the actual sanctuary is at the top of the pyramid, its entrance decorated by two massive serpentine columns. In the background is the Temple of the Jaguars.

195 (top) At the summit of the Castillo the sanctuary still contains a chacmool and a wonderful throne in the form of a jaguar, set with discs of jade, with eyes of pyrite and fangs of bone.

195 (above) The interior of the sanctuary of the Castillo is divided into three naves with a roof supported by pillars which carry traces of relief decoration.

196–197 (above) The vast ball court at Chichén Itzá is 146 m (480 ft) long and 36 m (118 ft) wide—the largest ball court in Mesoamerica. The field of play is flanked by vertical walls on which are fixed the hoops for scoring.

196 (right) Players of the ball game had to pass the rubber ball through these small hoops without using their hands to score points. This would have been extremely difficult and probably rather rare. This hoop is carved in relief with a writhing serpent.

dominated by two great religious buildings, the "Castillo" and the "Temple of the Warriors." The former, possibly dedicated to the god Kukulcan, is a pyramid 30 m (98 ft) high on a square base. Completely enclosed within the visible structure is an earlier, smaller pyramid. Both have nine elegantly decorated *talud-tablero* tiers. Four imposing stairways, one on each side, lead up to the sanctuary at the top. Each is composed of 91 steps; presumably not a random number as the sum of all four, including the continuous step around the base of the pyramid, equals 365, the total of days in the solar calendar. The cosmological symbolism of the impressive structure is thus evident.

The Temple of the Warriors echoes the architecture of the most important buildings at Tula and was also dedicated to the god Kukulcan, here in his aspect as Venus, the "Morning Star." It is a massive pyramid on four levels, with the temple on the topmost tier reached by a long staircase, at the top of which is a chacmool. Next to the temple, the "Hall of a Thousand Columns" is all that remains of the grandiose hypostyle hall that once flanked the temple. Its stone columns probably once supported a flat roof made of perishable materials.

Here, too, as in the Castillo and other buildings at Chichén Itzá, the typical Maya pyramidal structure is joined by new elements—colonnades of pleasing delicacy and iconography relating to the military orders and the cult of the Feathered Serpent.

The Group of the Thousand Columns is articulated around a series of clearly defined spaces, each of which had a precise function:

197 (right) A detail of the tzompantli, *a copy in stone of the wooden racks on which the skulls of decapitated people were displayed. The victims of this macabre ritual were perhaps the losing players in the ball game or defeated enemies. Such racks have also been found in the city of Tula.*

197 (top) A view of the immense Chichén Itzá ball court, seen from the south and overlooked by the Temple of the Jaguars. Its size seems more appropriate for giants or gods than humans.

197 (below center) The sanctuary on the platform of the Temple of the Jaguars resembles that of the Castillo in form, with the entrance decorated with massive serpentine columns. A stone jaguar-shaped throne is located beneath the portico of the main façade.

197

consisting of a ball court, a large trapezoidal plaza, and an area probably used as a market.

Toltec society was highly militarized, with an army divided into the orders of the Jaguar, the Eagle, and the Coyote. This martial aspect is apparent in various forms of artistic expression found at Chichén Itzá. One example is a series of reliefs depicting eagles and jaguars devouring human hearts, and another in which triumphant warriors exhibit the skulls of their decapitated victims.

Iconography linked to the ancient sacrificial rituals of the Mesoamerican civilizations have thus been overlaid with the increasingly bloodthirsty

198 On precise dates rituals in honor of Venus were held on the Platform of the Cones. Venus was venerated in both its aspects of Morning and Evening Star.

198 (above) The so-called High-Priest's Tomb is a pyramidal building, recently restored. Below its foundations was discovered a well leading to a cave where human bones and precious objects were found.

customs typical of the Mexican peoples of the Post-Classic Period.

Chichén Itzá also contains what may be regarded as the most interesting astronomical observatory of the Maya world. The "Caracol" is a very unusual two-story building with a circular plan. It was built over a number of phases on two large, superimposed rectangular platforms. A dual staircase leads up to the observatory itself, the ground floor of which is composed of three concentric

198–199 (above) On the exterior of the "Platform of the Eagles" is a relief frieze depicting felines and eagles devouring human hearts. In the background is the principal façade of the Temple of the Jaguars, with its entrance portico.

199 (opposite below left) The Platform of the Eagles at Chichén Itzá is very similar to the altar, now almost completely destroyed, in the center of the main plaza at Tula— further evidence of Toltec cultural and architectural influence at Chichén Itzá.

199 (opposite below right) The Mercado, an elegant plaza bordered by cylindrical columns, was originally a market.

200 (below) The Caracol, a circular building, acted as an astronomical observatory.

200 (bottom) The so-called Red House, or Casa Colorada, is a very sober Puuc-style temple on a platform, topped by a roofcomb.

200–201 (right) The "Nunnery," or Casa de las Monjas, is the Chichén Itzá building most clearly influenced by the Puuc style. Its principal façade is ornately decorated with masks representing the god Chac and the Earth Monster.

cylinders separated one from the other by two circular corridors covered with a ring-shaped corbeled vault. Four doorways oriented to the cardinal points pierce the perimeter wall. In the internal wall there are four further doors that lead to the central chamber, in the middle of which rises a massive pillar with a tight spiral staircase, from which the name of the building derives. On the top floor were various windows, of which only three survive. These are positioned to allow the observation of the movements of the planet Venus and other astronomical events. According to some scholars, like other round buildings in Mexico, the "Caracol" was not only an observatory, but also a temple dedicated to the cult of the Feathered Serpent.

Chichén Itzá also contains a number of buildings in the Puuc style that recall those of Uxmal and other centers of the same period, although their decoration is more restrained. Among these buildings are the Red House and the "Nunnery." On the doorway of an elegant building joined to the latter is an interesting relief: within a round, spoked frame a figure wearing a feather headdress sits cross-legged. According to one theory this is an image of a deified ruler. The Temple of the Jaguars rises on one side of the largest of the city's thirteen ball courts, in fact it is the largest in the whole of Mesoamerica.

Chichén Itzá fell into decline from around AD 1200 and was replaced by Mayapán as the capital of the Maya-Toltec peoples. The Sacred Cenote, however, remained a destination for pilgrims even in the period of the Spanish Conquest.

201 (opposite below left) This great mask of the god Chac is a decorative element on the upper façade of the "Nunnery." The god's characteristic long curling nose and the circles around his eyes are clearly visible.

201 (opposite below right) The Sacred Cenote of Chichén Itzá is a well created by natural geological processes. Its dark waters received human sacrifices in the name of Chac. The Cenote was also considered an access to the Underworld.

202–203 (overleaf) A reconstruction of Chichén Itzá: in the foreground at the left, is the "Nunnery," with a group of minor buildings. Higher up are the Caracol and the High Priest's Tomb, and top right, the Ball Court, the Castillo, the Temple of the Warriors, and the Hall of the Thousand Columns.

TENOCHTITLAN, THE METROPOLIS ON THE LAKE

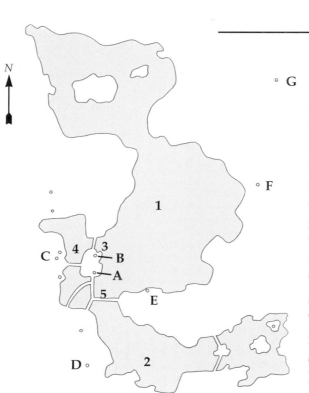

A Tenochtitlan
B Tlatelolco
C Tlacopan
D Cuicuilco
E Ixtapalapa
F Texcoco
G Teotihuacan

1 Lake Texcoco
2 Lake Xochimilco
3 Tepeyac Dam
4 Tlacopan Dam
5 Ixtapalapa Dam

Approaching Lake Texcoco for the first time, the Conquistadores led by Hernán Cortés were faced with the spectacle of a vast and wonderful metropolis in the area where Mexico City, the sprawling capital of the nation of the same name, now stands. This was Tenochtitlan, the capital of the Aztec empire, with its twin city Tlatelolco, separated by a brief stretch of water and linked by a bridge. Today all that remains are a few ruins in the center of the chaotic Mexican capital. A fascinating way of getting to know the ancient city of Tenochtitlan

is by exploring it first through the accounts of the Conquistadores and the ancient Aztec codices.

The first part of the Codex Mendoza deals with the story of Tenochtitlan up to the Spanish Conquest. Traditionally founded in AD 1324 by a leader named Tenoch, the city flourished in the remarkably brief period of 194 years, reaching the height of its glory under the rule of the last independent Aztec emperor, Motecuhzoma II.

Thus, on 8 November, 1519, the Spaniards met with a totally unexpected sight—a fabulous city that, as Bernal Díaz del Castillo recorded, seemed to some of the soldiers "to be nothing but a dream."

Tenochtitlan and Tlatelolco rose on a number of small islands linked to the mainland by long causeways, with access limited to just three gateways or by canoe, which gave the Aztec capital the appearance of an impregnable fortified city. At that time the twin centers had a staggeringly large population of 200,000 to 300,000 souls.

Established in a natural lake setting, Tenochtitlan was surrounded by a belt of *chinampas*, artificial islands made by covering frameworks of reeds with earth, anchored by willows. When a *chinampa* began to sink it was covered with another layer of earth, becoming increasingly fertile terrain for cultivation.

204–205 The cult of Quetzalcoatl was of great significance to the Aztec people. This polychrome stone serpent is located close to the Templo Mayor.

205 (above) Several anthropomorphic stone statues were found still leaning against the stairway of the Templo Mayor. They have been identified as standard-bearers.

205 (right, above) This chacmool, dated to around AD 1390, was originally located on the platform of the sanctuary of Tlaloc in the Templo Mayor.

205 (above) A tzompantli, a stone copy of the skull rack used to display the skulls of sacrificial victims, in the courtyard to the north of the Templo Mayor.

206–207 (overleaf) A reconstruction of the capital of the Aztec empire at the time of the Spanish Conquest. In the middle of the ceremonial center is the Templo Mayor, topped by the dual sanctuaries; the round temple in front is dedicated to the god of the wind.

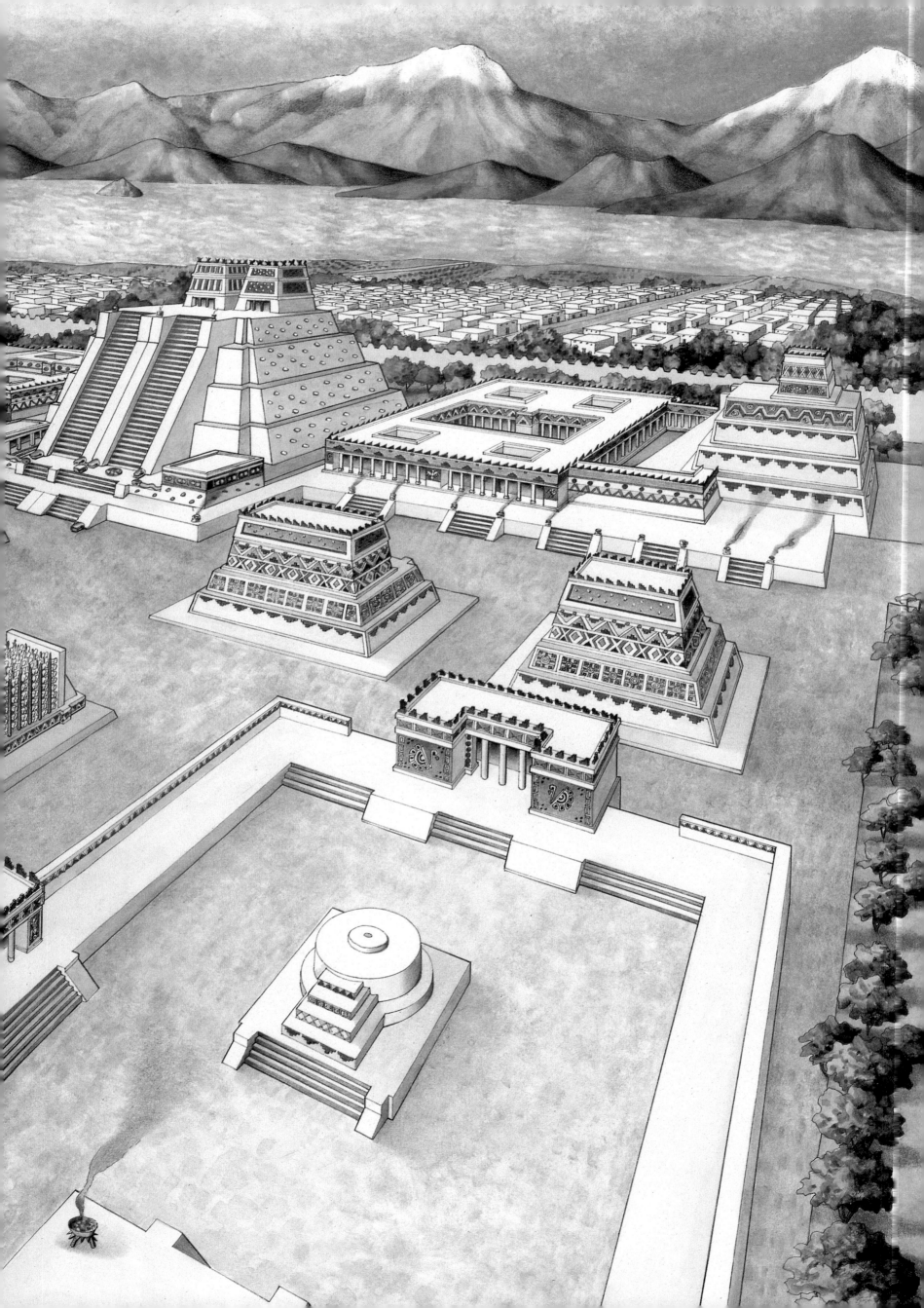

208 (left) Burning incense and other aromatic substances was a common Aztec practice. This polychrome terra-cotta censer from the Templo Mayor of Tenochtitlan represents the god of maize and dates from around AD 1470.

208 (center) A superb "Eagle Warrior," made of terra-cotta and dated to around AD 1480: Aztec soldiers, like the Toltecs, belonged to various military orders, among which were those of the Eagles and the Jaguars.

208 (below left) This great circular stone, 3 m (almost 10 ft) in diameter, was found on Platform IV of the Templo Mayor. The macabre scene carved in relief on its surface depicts the decapitation and dismembering of the goddess Coyolxauhqui by her brother Huitzilopochtli.

Tenochtitlan was thus criss-crossed by innumerable canals, along which the inhabitants moved with ease in their canoes, inspiring inevitable comparisons with Venice. Bernal Díaz's descriptions written in the 16th century are particularly evocative and useful. The city was subdivided into four quarters with the sacred area at the center, in keeping with the Aztec cosmogonic concept of the universe. Mingling with the neat residential quarters of the ordinary people were temples, palaces, ball courts, schools, and steam baths. One feature that particularly captured the imagination of the Spaniards as they approached the city was the number of gardens, brimming with tropical flowers and embellished with fountains. There

208–209 (right) The Templo Mayor was razed to the ground in the destruction of Tenochtitlan by Hernán Cortés in AD 1521, but the Aztec codices and remains brought to light by archaeologists have allowed the great religious building to be reconstructed here, as it might have appeared at the time of Motecuhzoma II. A vast complex of stairways gave access to the twin sanctuaries dedicated to Tlaloc and Huitzilopochtli. At the base of the platform were large statues covered with polychrome stucco depicting frogs and feathered serpents.

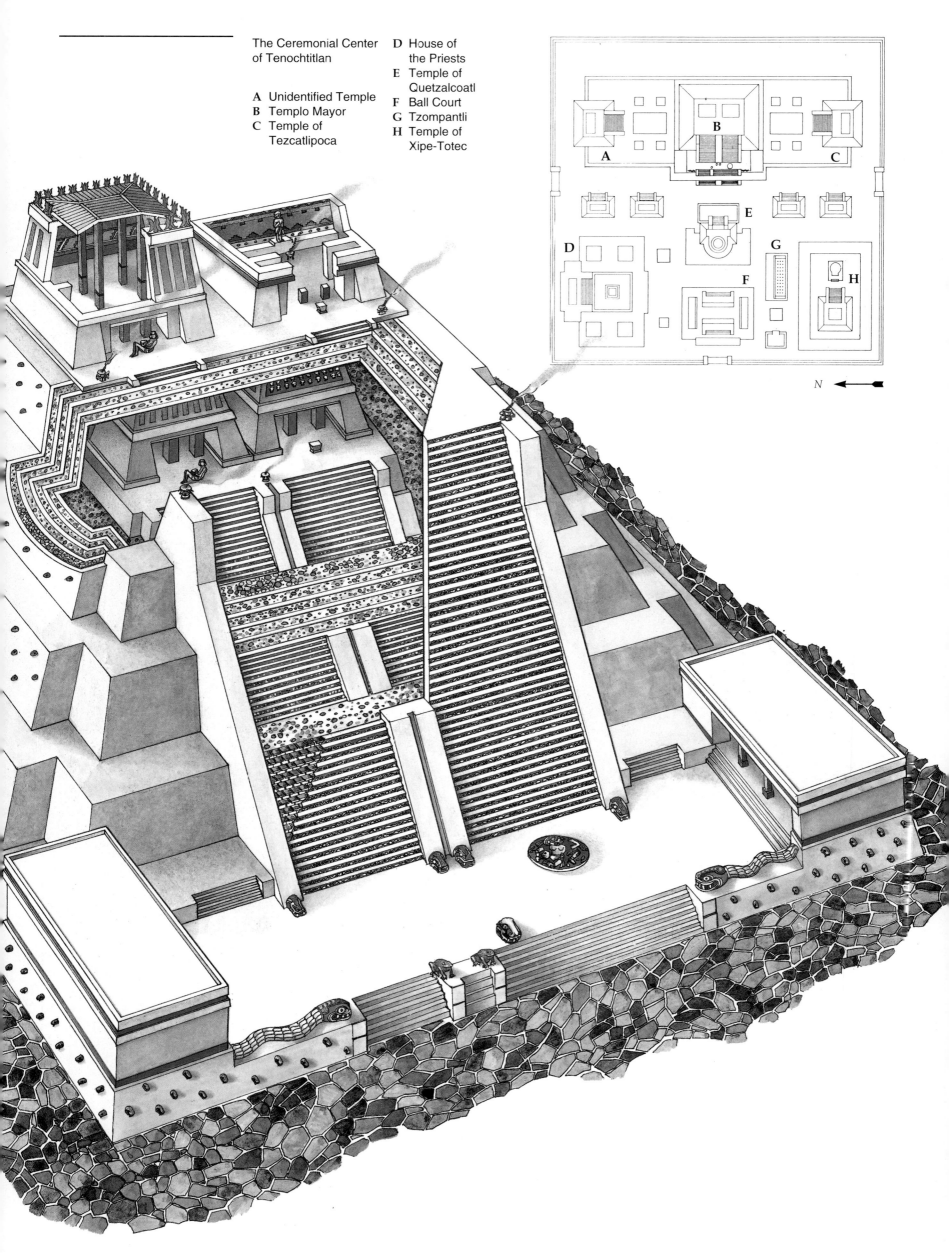

The Ceremonial Center of Tenochtitlan

A Unidentified Temple
B Templo Mayor
C Temple of Tezcatlipoca
D House of the Priests
E Temple of Quetzalcoatl
F Ball Court
G Tzompantli
H Temple of Xipe-Totec

N

were also numerous zoos where the nobles kept animals and birds.

Tlatelolco, Tenochtitlan's twin city, also surprised the Europeans with its huge market—which could contain some 60,000 people—where goods arrived by water. It dealt in all kinds of commodities: maize, cacao, rabbits, turkeys, wood, honey, silver, feathers, and even slaves. Trade was conducted by bartering or the use of cacao beans as currency. Buying and selling were strictly controlled by a college of magistrates and a police force.

Aztec codices and accounts of the Colonial era provide numerous descriptions and images of the principal monuments of the great Aztec metropolis, to which can be added the evidence of clay models of temple buildings. In the heart of the ceremonial center, in the Central Plaza, stood the most important sacred building, the "Templo Mayor," as it was called by the Spaniards. This imposing pyramidal building was only finished in AD 1487 and was composed of four or five floors rising

211 (opposite) One Aztec deity was Coatlicue, whose name means "Serpent Skirt." She was the goddess of the earth and fertility. In Aztec mythology, Coatlicue gave birth to Huitzilopochtli and Coyolxauhqui. This fearsome stone sculpture, found in 1780 in Mexico City, represents the goddess with a head formed of serpents and combining features of a bird of prey. Her necklace is made of skulls and human limbs, testifying to the fierce Aztec sacrificial rites.

210 (top right) This clay statue, found in the area of the Templo Mayor, probably depicts an Aztec warrior.

210 (center) Carved from greenstone, this impressive head again depicts Coyolxauhqui, whose name means "Decorated with Rattles."

210 (right) The eagle was a totemic bird for the Aztecs, linked to the story of the founding of Tenochtitlan. This majestic bird is carved from stone. This important object was found in 1978 in the area of the Templo Mayor.

"Sun Stone" were found. Following the discovery of these first traces of the ancient civilization, intellectual curiosity led to further research. Early in 20th century new excavations brought to light a corner of the stone base of the Templo Mayor; some years later part of the staircase leading up from the base and the remains of the *tzompantli* were also discovered. The stratigraphy of the great religious building was virtually completed by the late 1970s and some thousands of artifacts had been recovered.

In the area where ancient Tlatelolco once stood, in the square now known as the Plaza de las Tres Culturas, a series of excavations brought to light the remains of the great ceremonial area at the center of which rises the imposing stepped pyramid that was also dedicated to Huitzilopochtli and Tlaloc. It was from the top of this temple that the soldiers of Bernal Díaz contemplated Tenochtitlan, the last capital of Pre-Columbian Mexico.

212 (opposite) Xochipilli, the "Prince of Flowers," was an Aztec god of flowers, spring, and love. His cult was also linked to the ritual ball game. This stone sculpture shows him as a young man sitting on a throne with his legs crossed.

213 (left, above) A view of the sacred center of Tlatelolco, the twin city of Tenochtitlan, and originally the home of a vast market. In the middle rises a great pyramidal complex with dual sanctuaries, behind which is the baroque church of St. James of Tlatelolco.

213 (left, below) In the background on the left of this view of part of the ceremonial center of Tlatelolco is the Temple of the Numbers. Its walls were completely covered with glyphs relating to numbers and the days of the Ritual Calendar. On the right is the platform of the temple dedicated to the god of wind.

213 (below) An elegant example of Aztec sculpture: a bust, 70 cm (27½ in) high, portraying an Eagle Warrior. The facial features are extremely clear and realistic, unusual in Aztec art.

to a height of 30 m (98 ft). A very steep stairway led to a platform at the summit where twin sanctuaries were located. The first was dedicated to Huitzilopochtli, the ferocious tribal god of the Aztecs, and the second to the god of rain, Tlaloc. Terrible images have survived that show how the bodies of sacrificial victims, after their hearts had been ripped out in honor of the gods, were thrown down the steps as the crowds in the square in front of the pyramid stood and watched.

What remains today of this magnificent capital, of its majestic ceremonial center, and of the greatest emporium in Mexico? On 13 August, 1521, after having the emperor Motecuhzoma II assassinated, Cortés and his soldiers razed the fabulous city to the ground, destroying the very foundations of the monuments in order to construct new buildings and houses in the Colonial style. Three centuries later, in the Plaza de las Armas at Mexico City, a stone statue of the goddess Coatlicue and the famous

CACAXTLA, AN UNRESOLVED ENIGMA

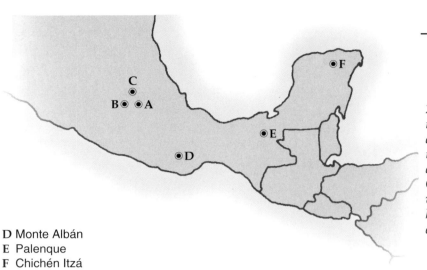

A Cacaxtla
B Tenochtitlan
C Teotihuacan
D Monte Albán
E Palenque
F Chichén Itzá

214 (below) Among the very fine wall decorations found at the site of Cacaxtla, dating to the late Classic Period, is this warrior wearing a headdress and earrings.

215 (opposite) In another scene from a Cacaxtla mural, a priest is depicted with eagle attributes, standing on a feathered serpent, perhaps the god Quetzalcoatl.

214 (below) The freshness and richness of the colors seen here are characteristic of the murals of Cacaxtla. This scene depicts a priest, with a jaguar costume and feet, standing on a serpent-jaguar.

Around AD 800, when the power of Teotihuacan and the Maya cities of the Classic Period was in decline, a number of sites began to flourish in central Mexico and regional cultures developed, though they were still under the shadow of the legacies of neighboring civilizations. Among these new centers were Xochicalco, Cholula, and Cacaxtla. Cacaxtla, in the Mexican state of Tlaxcala, flourished between around AD 650 and 900, its ceremonial center dominated by a

view of the peak of the volcano Iztaccihuatl.

Cacaxtla is the name given to the site by the Aztecs when they conquered the area; in Nahuatl it means "The Place of the Cacaxtli," a *cacaxtli* being a trader's pack. Various clues have led to the suggestion that the group that founded the original nucleus of the city belonged to the Olmec-Xicallanca, a community of merchants from the Gulf Coast.

Cacaxtla is particularly important for its magnificent and abundant wall paintings, considered by scholars to be the most significant and complete in central Mexico. In quality they perhaps surpass even those of Teotihuacan. The cycle of frescoes, with many details that are Maya in style, in part illustrates scenes of warfare. This theme, with an emphasis on cruel and bloody aspects, is foreign to the iconography of Teotihuacan, which concentrates on the religious sphere. The figures, sumptuously dressed warriors and defeated prisoners, are depicted with great realism in bright hues and are almost life-size. Alongside the martial scenes, the frescoes of Cacaxtla include some with mythological themes. Among these are depictions of two figures, one on either side of a

215

Mexico. Some of the glyphic symbols in the frescoes can be compared with those of Teotihuacan, and others with those of the Zapotecs and Mixtecs of Oaxaca. At present these symbols have not been deciphered.

Excavations have recently brought to light more paintings, the iconography of which again concentrates on war and reveals the warrior aspect of this society of merchants who dominated the Mexican plateau between the 7th and the 10th century. Perhaps the aim of the wars was to take the greatest number of prisoners for sacrifice, as practiced later by the Aztecs.

217 (left, below) In the Cacaxtla frescoes many mythological creatures appear, such as this monstrous being with serpentine and feline features.

217 (below) Turtles, deer, and numerous other animals are featured in the frescoes discovered to date. These images are remarkable both for their superb artistry and their excellent state of preservation.

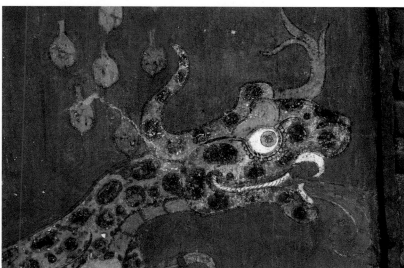

216 (opposite) A warrior of terrifying appearance, depicted in a war scene in the cycle of wall paintings at Cacaxtla. The style resembles that of the Maya paintings of Bonampak.

217 (top) The iconography of the jaguar warrior represented here belongs to the cultural context of the Mexican plateau, but the style is typically Maya.

doorway, dressed in the costume of an eagle and a jaguar respectively, and also having attributes of each animal. These are particularly unusual and aesthetically very fine. The former, depicted in a struggle with a Feathered Serpent, raises further questions as to the place and date of origin of this cult.

The Cacaxtla frescoes are particularly interesting for the variety of cultural references which they contain. In style they have similarities with the wall paintings of the late Maya period at Bonampak; however, certain motifs are unique to central

218 (right) Perhaps an observatory, the four-story "Tower," is one of the most unusual buildings of the city of Palenque.

218 (far right) One of the courtyards surrounded by buildings composing the "Palace" complex at Palenque.

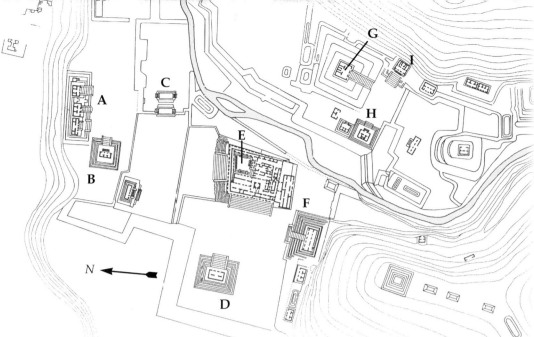

PALENQUE, THE PRIDE OF LORD PACAL

A Northern Temple Group
B Temple of the Count
C Ball Court
D Great Temple
E The Palace
F Temple of the Inscriptions
G Temple of the Cross
H Temple of the Sun
I Temple of the Foliated Cross

N

Palenque, in the Chiapas region, is today one of the best preserved Maya sites. It was also one of the first cities to be rediscovered after its centuries-long abandonment following a decline that began in the 9th century AD. In 1746, Padre Solis, a Spanish priest, was sent by his bishop on an exploratory journey to Santo Domingo de Palenque. He had heard rumors of ancient remains partially buried in the forest vegetation, and was greatly impressed by what he found. Solis was the first to report the existence of the ruins to the colonial authorities, but from then on numerous travelers and scholars were drawn to the mysterious city. For a long time, however, no one knew who built it.

Of the many who sketched the monuments, the work of Count Waldeck is worth particular mention. He had decided to study Mexican antiquities in depth and in 1825 began his tour at Palenque. Over the next year and a half he made the first excavations, studied, and drew the remains. His painstaking work in the form of numerous informative lithographs clearly reveals a subjective interpretation of the buildings and archaeological finds. The Count, like many other scholars of his era, could not conceive of the existence of an ancient civilization so far removed geographically from the context of the Classical world in Europe.

218–219 (left) The architectural complex at Palenque known as the Palace, composed of long buildings around internal courtyards, was perhaps the administrative center of the ruling caste.

219 (right, above) A jade plaque found in the funeral crypt of Lord Pacal who died in AD 683. Its relief decoration depicts a noble wearing a feathered headdress.

219 This carved stucco frieze was once covered with paint, of which no trace remains today. Together with other friezes it formed a decorative element in the Palace at Palenque.

220–221 (overleaf) An evocative image of the platform and buildings comprising the Palace at Palenque—it captures some of the appeal and mystery of the site.

222 (opposite above, left and right) The Temple of the Cross and the Temple of the Foliated Cross at Palenque were both built in AD 692, in the reign of King Chan Bahlum, son of Lord Pacal.

Frederick Catherwood also produced beautiful images of the ruins of the city of Palenque. He meticulously copied the inscriptions found on the stelae and other monuments though no one at the time could read them. They have since been deciphered, providing us with much knowledge of the history of this Classic Period Maya site.

The oldest constructions at Palenque were commissioned by the ruler who was the first to promote the political and cultural development of the city: the texts recount that his name was Pacal, which in Maya means "Shield."

222–223 Palenque is arguably one of the most beautiful of Maya sites. This is a view of the principal religious buildings, seen from the Temple of the Cross. To the left is the Temple of the Sun, built in AD 692, close to the ruins of other temple buildings. In the background is the great Temple of the Inscriptions, beneath which was the tomb of Lord Pacal.

Pacal's rule over Palenque was a long one, from AD 615 to 683, and the oldest parts of the so-called "Palace" date from this era. The Palace is an architectural complex set on a large platform, composed of numerous buildings grouped around courtyards, inside two of which were other constructions. Although the name "Palace" suggests a residential complex, perhaps the home of the royal family, it may also have been the setting for religious and cultural ceremonies. The great four-story tower rising above the Palace could have been a watchtower or, more probably, an astronomical observatory.

Near the Palace is Palenque's most impressive structure, the Temple of the

223 (above) A detail of the summit of the Temple of the Sun, built by Chan Bahlum in AD 692. It is decorated with relief sculptures and crowned by a roofcomb. Together with the Temples of the Cross and the Foliated Cross, the Temple of the Sun forms the so-called "Group of the Cross."

Inscriptions. Count Waldeck was fascinated by the symbols inscribed on the stonework embellishing the central room, and transcribed them, hoping to arrive at an understanding of their meaning. However, his interpretation of the symbols was highly subjective—he even saw in them stylized heads of elephants.

The Temple of the Inscriptions is important for more than the beauty of its architecture, however. In 1952 the Mexican archaeologist Alberto Ruz discovered a great secret concealed within it. Hidden by slabs in the floor of the temple on the top of the pyramid, he found the entrance to a long staircase leading down through the platform. At the bottom was a large crypt with a high corbeled ceiling.

Within this Funerary Crypt lay a monolithic sarcophagus covered with a great slab, weighing over 5 tons, and decorated with reliefs and inscriptions. Ruz immediately realized that the sarcophagus contained the remains of a high-ranking figure, certainly a king, who was buried with a fabulous funerary treasure. The inscriptions on the sarcophagus have revealed that the illustrious person was none other than the famous Pacal, whose eternal rest had been assured for centuries.

A superb funerary mask of jade, with eyes of shell and obsidian, was placed over the face of the king; among the objects making up the treasure were two very realistic stucco heads, one of which is perhaps a portrait of Pacal. The lid of the sarcophagus is surely the most intensively studied Maya artifact. Its low relief scene—read vertically and surrounded by a band of symbols of the sky, stars, the sun, and the moon—is highly complex.

Its central iconography illustrates the passage of the king from earthly life to the spiritual world: he is depicted "falling" downward into the gaping jaws of an "earth monster," which represents the Underworld. Above and behind Pacal is the Cosmic Tree, on whose cruciform shape a fantastic bird perches. Such symbolism represents the link between the Underworld, the kingdom of the dead, and the Upper World, the home of the gods. The double-headed serpent around the cross-branches testifies to the royal lineage of the deceased. Certain American scholars have recently put forward a new interpretation of the rich iconography of the relief scene and the elements that compose it.

224–225 and 224 (opposite below left) The Temple of the Inscriptions at Palenque stands on a platform of eight tiers. In 1952, Mexican archaeologist Alberto Ruz discovered below its foundations the tomb of Lord Pacal, who had been buried with a sumptuous funerary treasure.

224 (opposite below right) In the plaza in front of the Temple of the Inscriptions stands a small altar, which reproduces in miniature the form of the sacred building behind it.

225 (top) Palenque also contains other impressive complexes of a religious nature. This is the Temple of the Count, a structure of modest size built during the reign of Lord Pacal.

225 At the northern end of the ceremonial center of Palenque, close to the Temple of the Count, stands a pyramidal complex known as the Northern Group, consisting of small temple buildings on a platform.

226 (below) At the time of its discovery, the steep flight of steps leading to the burial chamber of King Pacal was completely filled with rubble, which was meticulously cleared by archaeologists.

226–227 This reconstruction shows the position of the Funerary Crypt and the flights of access steps, hidden in the body of the Temple of the Inscriptions. The temple on the pyramid has been cut away to reveal its interior.

227 (left) A huge heavy triangular slab of stone sealed the crypt, which Alberto Ruz was finally able to enter in 1952, after three years spent clearing the rubble from the access stairway.

227 (below) A drawing of lid of the sarcophagus shows Lord Pacal being swallowed by the earth monster; behind him is the Tree of Life in the branches of which a bird-serpent perches.

227 (left) The sarcophagus, which weighs over 5 tons, is only slightly smaller than the burial chamber, suggesting that it was put in position before the crypt and the pyramid itself were built.

228–229 (overleaf) A panoramic view of the pyramids making up the so-called "Group of the Cross" at Palenque; from left to right: the Temple of the Cross, the Temple of the Foliated Cross, Temple XIV, and the Temple of the Sun.

230 *Placed over the face of Lord Pacal himself, this life-size jade mask was just one element of his rich funerary treasure.*

231 *(opposite) One of two stucco portrait heads found in the tomb of Lord Pacal. The face, whose features express serenity and wisdom, and the sumptuous headdress probably of feathers, a symbol of power and nobility in the context of the Mayan civilization, suggest that we may be looking at a portrait of Pacal himself.*

In a thought-provoking reading, these scholars interpret the images as an astronomical code, according to which the Cosmic Tree is the Milky Way, the "White Road" along which the spirit of the dead king traveled before being reborn in a new life.

The inscriptions narrate that Pacal was succeeded on the throne of Palenque by his son Chan Bahlum, "Serpent Jaguar." It was he who ordered the construction of the three great temples forming the so-called "Group of the Cross," consisting of the Temple of the Sun, the Temple of the Cross, and the Temple of the Foliated Cross. These temples, located at the top of pyramidal structures and crowned with typical roofcombs, were not positioned randomly; rather, their orientations were linked to Maya religious ideology and cosmogony. Each was also decorated with reliefs, which in the Temple of the Sun include the mask of the sun god in his nocturnal aspect embodied as the jaguar.

The inscriptions of Palenque have provided a wealth of fascinating information about the dynastic history of the descendants of Pacal. For example, it has been established that the succession to the throne at one time passed through the maternal line, a very rare occurrence in the Maya world.

An interesting inscription also concerns the dedicatory ceremony for the Temple of the Cross held by Chan Bahlum. The young king chose to celebrate the event at a particular moment in the year when three planets were in conjunction with the sun. This once more demonstrates the enormous importance that the Maya gave to astronomical events.

BONAMPAK, CITY OF THE PAINTED WARRIORS

232–233 Bonampak is a small Maya center dating from the late 8th century AD, celebrated for its "Temple of the Paintings." Here the temple has been reconstructed with the walls cut away to reveal the interior. The frescoes decorating the three adjoining rooms are,

with those of Cacaxtla, the most beautiful discovered in Mesoamerica and probably commemorate the victories of a great leader.

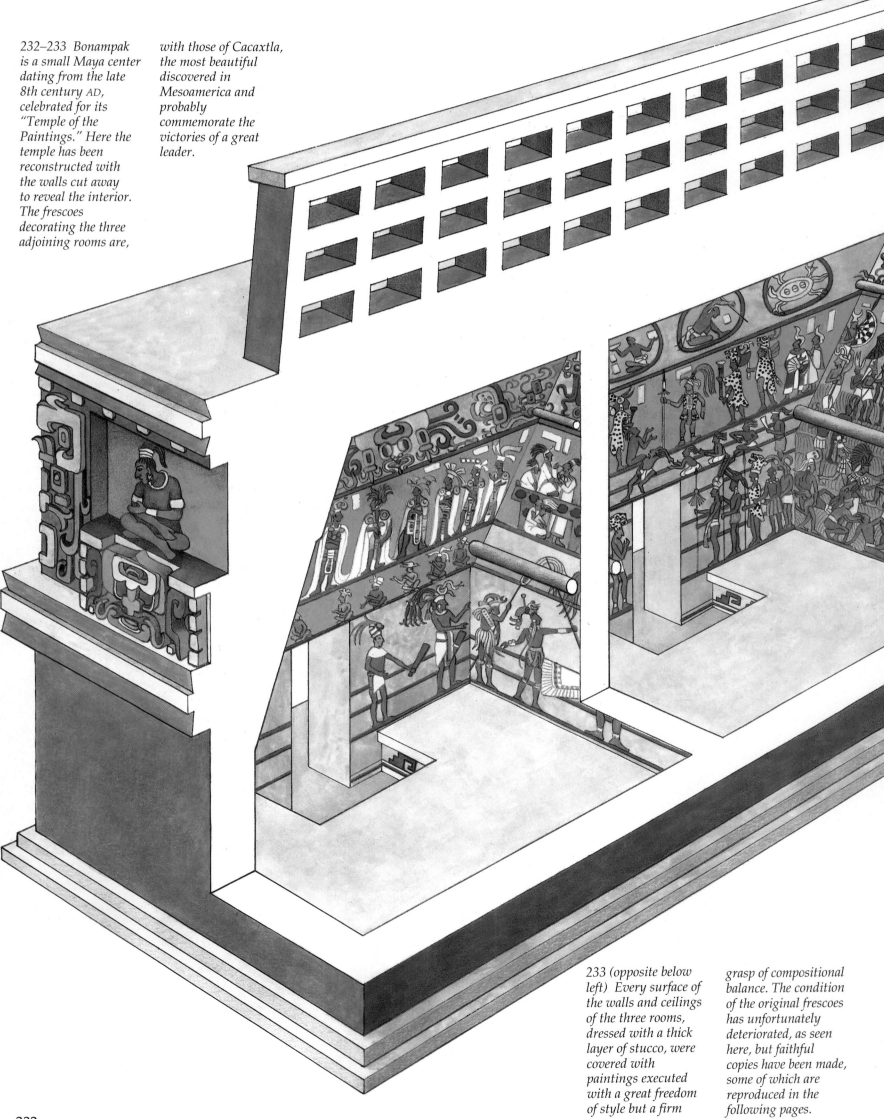

233 (opposite below left) Every surface of the walls and ceilings of the three rooms, dressed with a thick layer of stucco, were covered with paintings executed with a great freedom of style but a firm

grasp of compositional balance. The condition of the original frescoes has unfortunately deteriorated, as seen here, but faithful copies have been made, some of which are reproduced in the following pages.

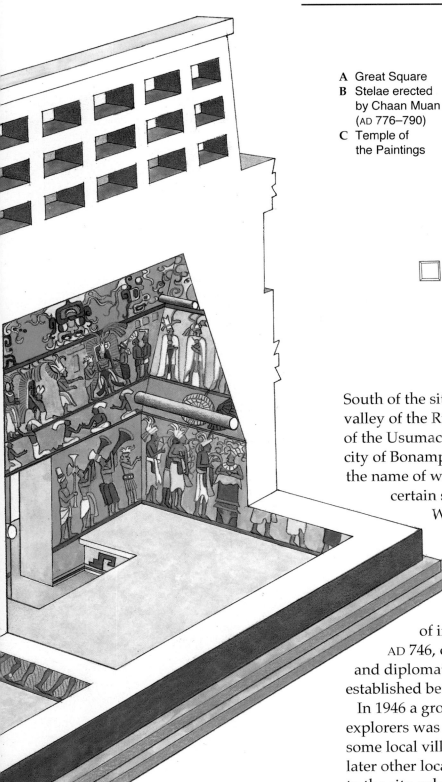

A Great Square
B Stelae erected
  by Chaan Muan
  (AD 776–790)
C Temple of
  the Paintings

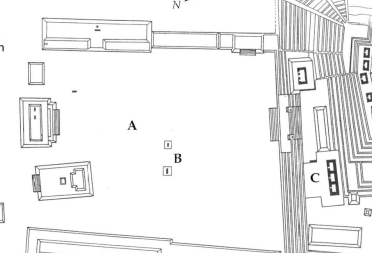

N

A

B

C

233 (right above)
The acropolis on
which the "Temple of
the Paintings" stands
overlooks a plaza, once
surrounded by
platforms and
buildings.

233 (right below)
One of the three stelae
erected at Bonampak
by Chaan Muan, the
ruler who came to the
throne of the city in
AD 776.

South of the site of Yaxchilán, in the valley of the Río Lacanhá, a tributary of the Usumacinta, lie the ruins of the city of Bonampak. This small center, the name of which according to certain scholars means "Painted Walls," was tied in some way to Yaxchilán, and both reached their peak during the early Classic Period as indicated by a number of inscriptions. One, dated AD 746, cites a form of political and diplomatic alliance that was established between the two cities.

In 1946 a group of American explorers was led to Bonampak by some local villagers, and a few months later other locals led a photographer to the site, who was the first to discover the fabulously frescoed rooms of a structure—the most glorious example of Maya wall painting yet found. Three adjacent rooms within the "Temple of Paintings" have stuccoed walls and ceilings frescoed with polychrome scenes of a historical nature that display great artistic skill.

In Room 1 the central theme revolves around ritual preparations for war, with the king surrounded by a large group of ladies, courtiers, and musicians. The magnificence of the court is displayed in the richly decorated clothes and headdresses worn by the various figures, while the dancers wear feathered backracks made with green quetzál feathers. Nearby, other figures wear monstrous masks; one of them is equipped with

crayfish pincers, another is disguised as a crocodile, and a third personifies the god of maize. Accompanying the dancers are musicians playing trumpets, drums, and percussion instruments made of tortoise shells.

The murals of Room 2 instead concentrate on the theme of a victory, following a bloody battle, achieved by a ruler who is depicted flanked by his aides. The well-armed warriors have captured numerous enemies who are shown without weapons or ornaments. Prostrating themselves at the feet of the victors, the defeated prisoners are depicted in postures of submission: one of them seems to beg

234 (left) A view of the west wall of Room 1 at Bonampak. A procession of dancers and musicians moves against a turquoise background.

234–235 The frescoes at Bonampak provide a wealth of details of Maya costumes of the Classic Period. This scene shows warriors equipped with lances and rectangular shields and wearing eye-catching headdresses covered with feathers or in the shape of animal heads.

for mercy, others lie wounded and bleeding. The paintings may record an actual event that took place probably around AD 790, and the ruler depicted in his moment of triumph was Chaan Muan. His coronation was in AD 776, as recorded on a commemorative stela. From the epigraphic texts we know that this king married a princess from Yaxchilán. At Bonampak, therefore, we have in the wall paintings the pictorial version of events found also in the historical testimony of the writings.

Room 3 contains paintings which complete the historical cycle. Here Chaan Muan is seen celebrating his victory together with members of his court and family in a sumptuous ceremony. The festivities conclude with a sacrificial ritual in which the victims are offered to the gods. As well as the stelae mentioned above, a number of inscriptions on the doorways of the structure with the wall paintings fill out our knowledge of the history and chronology of the reign of Chaan Muan.

Unfortunately, the brilliant paintings of Bonampak, protected for centuries by the total darkness of the chambers, have lost much of their original splendor. Faithful copies were made, however, in exact replicas of the original building, that can be seen both in the Museum of Anthropology at Mexico City and the Florida State Museum, Gainesville.

234 (center) A detail from a mural of a violent fighting in a battle during the reign of Chaan Muan.

234 This detail from the fresco in Room 2 depicts an horrific scene in which a warrior clothed in a jaguar skin decapitates a captured enemy. Inscriptions show that such wars did take place.

236 (right) Yaxchilán was one of the great Maya centers of the Classic Period, located in the valley of the Usumacinta river. This view is of the principal Plaza where numerous monuments can be seen.

236–237 The three main temples of Yaxchilán were built on terraced platforms amidst the lush tropical vegetation.

YAXCHILAN,
A VIBRANT URBAN SCENE

A Great Square
B Building 33

1 East terrace
2 West terrace
3 South Group

Yaxchilán, rediscovered in 1881, is sited in the valley of the river Usumacinta, close to the border between the modern countries of Mexico and Guatemala. The city flourished in the Classic Period and its architecture is stylistically very similar to that of Palenque. Among the common elements are stone-faced walls, broad staircases, and large, pierced roofcombs—decorative elements on the tops of buildings. Unfortunately very little is left of the sophisticated stucco decorations that once covered them, as they have been eroded by wind, rain, and the encroaching vegetation.

Most of Yaxchilán's buildings were erected on terraces in two groups. The palaces have a rectangular structure and many of them contain dual rows of rooms with access by three doors. Monuments in the form of stelae, altars, and lintels have elaborate relief decorations accompanied by inscriptions. In the 1960s epigraphist Tatiana Proskouriakoff began a long process of deciphering the Maya glyphs. Finally, a breakthrough enabled her to interpret the symbols in the inscribed texts, thus opening a window on the mystery of the Maya writing system. She discovered that the texts had a historical theme and celebrated the acts of rulers and the most important events in their lives, accompanied by precise dates and calendric computations.

Today we know that for many years Yaxchilán was ruled by kings of a single dynasty. The most celebrated were "Bird Jaguar," "Shield Jaguar," and his wife "Lady Xoc," commemorated in many of the reliefs.

237 (below, center) A broad stairway leads to the top of one of the platforms facing onto the main square of Yaxchilán. Many buildings in the city have large and elegant roofcombs, the majority of which have, unfortunately, been eroded. Friezes and inscriptions decorate the lintels of the palaces.

237 (bottom) The temples and the "palaces" of Yaxchilán were built in a style characteristic of the Usumacinta valley, with friezes covered with stucco decorating the upper sections and elegant roofcombs.

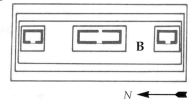

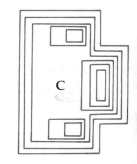

UAXACTUN, THE OBSERVATORY OF THE SUN

Plan of Complex E at Uaxactún

A Pyramid E-VII-sub
B East Complex
C Group A-5

Uaxactún, in Guatemala, was an important center in the Late Preclassic period in the Maya lowlands. It shares elements in common—such as pyramidal structures and early ball courts with a primitive rectangular shape—with other great sites of the end of the Preclassic, including El Mirador in the same region and Lamanai and Cerros in Belize. The ceremonial buildings at these sites were platforms, initially of beaten earth and subsequently of stone, composed of superimposed rectangular steps, the dimensions of which decreased toward the top. Large stucco masks depicting monstrous beings were placed on the terraces as decorative elements flanking the stairways. A central stairway led to the summit of the pyramid where the true sanctuary was located. In some cases traces of the foundations and walls of the sanctuary remain, but they would originally have had a thatched roof.

Uaxactún, the name of which means "Eight Stones," lies a short distance from Tikal in the tropical lowlands of the Petén region. The heart of the city was composed of groups of buildings set on the slopes of hills, which over time were transformed into large complexes. In the surrounding area

238–239 The most famous monument at Uaxactún is the "observatory," a pyramid with four stairways built in the Preclassic Period, known as E-VII-sub. It was subsequently incorporated into another building, which was dismantled to expose this structure. Its role was related to the solstices and the equinoxes.

238 (opposite below left) The ceremonial center of Uaxactún lies in the Petén region of present day Guatemala. It flourished from the middle of the Preclassic Period to the 10th century AD. This view is of the remains of a temple complex of modest size, labeled Group B.

238 (opposite below right) Group A at Uaxactún was a complex of important buildings built over five centuries between the early 4th century and the beginning of the 9th. Here, the imposing ruins of "Palace 5" stand at the top of a massive platform.

239 (top) The great east Square of Group A at Uaxactún is dominated by the imposing bulk of Building 18, the ruins of a vast, elongated building, set on top of the stepped platform.

239 Although it is smaller in size, Building E 10 recalls the pyramidal complex at Tikal. Numerous stylistic analogies exist between Tikal and Uaxactún, sites which developed simultaneously.

240 *This drawing shows the lines of sight used by the priests of Uaxactún for their astronomical observations. From a fixed point on the pyramid, points of reference pass through the axis of the building perpendicular to it, and the external corners of two other buildings, aligned with the principal movements of the sun—the summer solstice, the equinoxes, and the winter solstice respectively.*

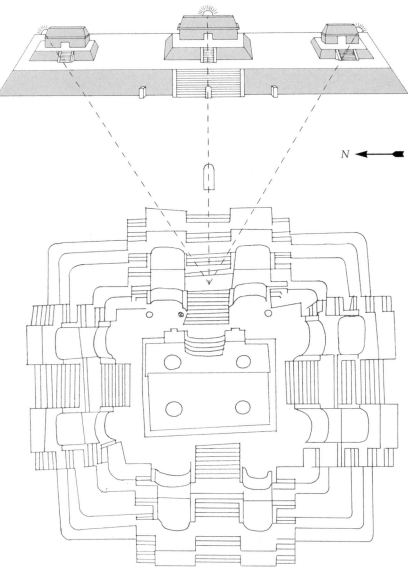

N ←

the scattered rural houses were built of perishable materials, and only their stone foundations have survived.

Perhaps the most significant building at Uaxactún is so-called "Pyramid E," uncovered by the celebrated archaeologist Sylvanus Morley beneath the ruins of later structures. Three phases of construction have been distinguished, that spanned the last centuries before Christ, making this one of the oldest pyramids to have been discovered in this region. The earliest structure which is the one now visible, is known as Pyramid E-VII-sub. It is a fairly low building, dominated by four massive stairways flanked by large stucco and stone masks, possibly depicting the Jaguar God of the Underworld, or a form of earth monster of Olmec origin. Postholes on the top indicate the existence of a superstructure made of perishable materials.

In the Classic Period a new pyramid that has subsequently been removed was built over the original structure.

Together with a platform located on the east side which was crowned by three small temples, it constituted a complex that acted as an astronomical observatory. From the summit of the pyramid the astronomers could observe the sun rising behind the central temple on the days of the autumn and spring equinoxes. The sun rose behind the right-hand temple on 21 December and behind the left-hand temple on 21 June, respectively the winter and summer solstices.

This astronomical function was also present in the earliest phase. According to one suggestion, the pyramid's "Maltese Cross" plan, similar to that of the Twin Pyramids of Tikal, reproduces the cruciform sign for Zero, that is to say, the symbol not only of "completion" but also of the universe subdivided into four quadrants plus the center. Interestingly the stucco masks decorating the pyramid also include depictions of the sky serpent.

240–241 The vivid colors of this reconstruction of Pyramid E-VII-sub at Uaxactún, built in the Preclassic Period, may seem surprising, but evidence was found on the stone to show that the building was once covered with polychrome stucco. Just like the Greek temples of the Classical period in Europe, those of Mesoamerica were painted in bright colors, most of which have disappeared over the centuries. Pyramid E-VII-sub is one of the oldest architectural structures of the Maya civilization. In the Classic Period it was incorporated into a similar, but larger structure of which today only traces remain. The four sides of the pyramid are decorated with great stucco masks resembling those of the Pyramid at Cerros in Belize. Their iconography is linked with the cults of the earth monster, the sun in its nocturnal aspect and other deities associated with the heavenly bodies.

242 (right) The summits of the highest of the pyramids of Tikal emerge from the dense tropical forest of Guatemala; Temples I, II, and V and the so-called Pyramid of the Lost World are visible.

242–243 (below) This view shows the upper part of the Pyramid of the Lost World and, behind it, the summit of the tallest building in Tikal, Temple IV, which rises with its roof comb to a height of 70 m (229 ft).

TIKAL, THE APOTHEOSIS OF MAYA PYRAMIDS

A Temple IV
B Complex N
C South Acropolis
D Plaza of the Seven Temples
E Temple III
F Complex O
G West Plaza
H Temple II
I Great Plaza

J North Acropolis
K Temple I
L Temple V
M East Plaza
N Central Acropolis
O Complex R
P Complex Q
Q Group F
R Group G

The temples of Tikal, the tallest and most impressive in the Maya world, rise above the dense tropical forest of Guatemala, presenting visitors with a remarkable vision of majesty. The history of the city is intensively documented by the epigraphic texts that indicate with precision the onset of its golden age and its subsequent decline. Stela 29 carries the oldest date, which corresponds to AD 292; while the most recent, on Stela 11, corresponds to AD 869.

A series of factors, including the strategic position of Tikal in the Maya cultural area and its historical development recorded on its monuments, have recently led epigraphers Nikolai Grube and Simon Martin to formulate a theory that Tikal and Calakmul together held a dominant position over other Maya city states of the Classic Period.

Numerous excavations carried out since 1881, and others still in progress in the area of Tikal, have brought to light around three thousand monuments, scattered over an area of no less than 15. 5 sq. km (6 sq. miles). At the heart of the city the true ceremonial center extends over a very large area—clearly this is a site of extraordinary importance from both an archaeological and a historical point of view. The ceremonial center is organized around a main plaza, the edges of which are crowded with a veritable "forest" of commemorative stelae and sacrificial altars.

The east and west sides of the main plaza are dominated by two twin constructions known respectively as Temple I and Temple II. In addition to these, other ceremonial buildings include the North, the South, and the Central Acropolis, the Plaza of the Seven Temples, a ball court, and reservoirs.

243 (top) The massive isolated structure of the Pyramid of the Lost World is almost hidden among the thick vegetation.

243 (center) As if floating in a green sea, the tops of the twin Temples I and II emerge from the jungle, one in front of the other.

244–245 (overleaf) A reconstruction of Tikal, the most extensive and perhaps the most powerful Maya city of the Classic Period. A number of reservoirs supplied the city and the surrounding countryside with water. A major road enabled villagers to reach the ceremonial center.

243

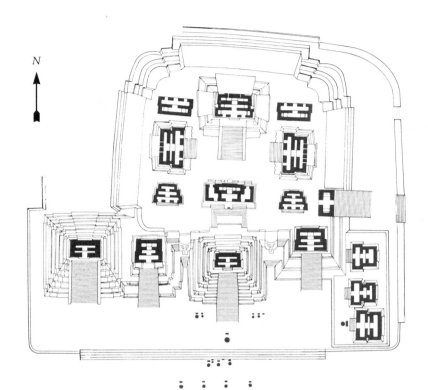

The majority of the buildings of the ceremonial center of Tikal can be dated to a period between AD 600 and 800. Epigraphic and archaeological sources have been used to reconstruct the history of the city, which has proved to be complex and filled with events linked to the dynasties that reigned for many centuries.

As early as AD 400, Tikal had achieved considerable cultural and economic development, fuelled by the strong influence of Teotihuacan. However, it has been established that from AD 537 what may be defined as a hiatus occurred, revealed by the total absence of inscriptions. From the 7th century AD Tikal enjoyed a revival, and commemorative stelae and prestigious new buildings were erected once again. From this moment the city began to flourish politically, economically, and culturally—a phase that lasted until the end of 9th century.

At Tikal, as at Palenque, archaeologists have brought to light remarkable tombs with rich funerary treasures concealed below the foundations of the ceremonial buildings. Precious objects, pottery vessels, and priceless masks of jade bear witness to the power of the dead person with whom they were buried. Among these were the rulers, with odd-sounding nicknames, whose portraits feature in complex reliefs and whose lives were recorded by the inscriptions. Among these the most

celebrated were Jaguar Paw, Stormy Sky, and also Curl Nose, during whose reign the inhabitants of the city numbered at least 40,000.

Sophisticated vase paintings found in the funerary treasures depict court life, with rulers and nobles dressed in sumptuous costumes, or scenes of everyday life. Iconographical study of these paintings has opened a window on the court life of one of the most powerful cities of Pre-Columbian Mesoamerica.

246 (above) Temple I, with its nine superimposed tiers, stands on the North Acropolis.

246–247 The great ceremonial center of Tikal is composed of numerous architectural complexes. This view is of Temple I, with the main plaza in the background.

247 (opposite below) A view from the top of the Central Acropolis, with Temple II visible in the background to the right.

Temples I and II at Tikal overlook the other complexes of the ceremonial center. The first rises to an imposing height of 50 m (164 ft) in nine levels, with an extremely steep stairway leading to the sanctuary at the summit. Entry to the sanctuary, which consists of three parallel rooms with corbeled ceilings, was permitted to members of the priesthood and the nobility only. The ordinary people attended the ceremonies from the facing square.

*248–249 (overleaf)
This reconstruction of Tikal gives some impression of its vastness and complexity. The twin pyramids, Temple I and Temple II, face onto the main plaza which is surrounded by other complexes such as the North Acropolis and the Central Acropolis, originally covered with painted stucco.*

250 (right) In front of the stepped platform of one of the twin pyramids forming Complex Q stand commemorative stelae, in some cases associated with altars or cylindrical thrones.

250–251 Like the other sacred buildings at Tikal, Temple II has an impressive roofcomb. At the base of the stairway, on the plaza, are stelae erected to celebrate the deeds of the rulers of the city.

251 (below) A great
stairway leads to the
summit of the
Pyramid of the Lost
World, a large temple
located in the
southwest tip of
Tikal's ceremonial
center.

251 (center) This
impressive "green
mountain" is actually
a pyramid still
covered with
vegetation: only part
of the great city of
Tikal has been rescued
from the continual
advance of the tropical
forest.

Temple I is crowned by an elegant roofcomb with cavities covered with vaults, designed to reduce the weight of the structure. Here, to a greater extent than elsewhere, the architectonic power and surprising dimensions of the sacred building clearly express the desire to create a kind of artificial "mountain," perhaps in the hope of reducing the distance between mortal man and the gods.

Facing Temple I, Temple II is similar in structure but more modest in size. The roofcombs that decorate the other pyramids, such as Temple III and Temple IV, emerge above the vegetation. In the central complex of buildings is an immense five-story palace, perhaps the residence of the nobility or an administrative center, composed of halls and galleries with corbeled ceilings. Stone benches and and remarkably well-preserved wooden beams can still be seen in these rooms.

Walking around the majestic monuments it is easy to imagine the powerful sovereign Curl Nose himself progressing through the rooms and conducting sacrifices, adorned with jewels and feathers, as illustrated in the vase paintings. Some questions and mysteries concerning this "metropolis in the jungle" have yet to be resolved, however.

From the numerous inscribed stelae found at Tikal we have learned of the history of a single, uninterrupted ruling dynasty that governed the city from the early Classic Period through to the 9th century: at least 32 kings succeeded one another to the throne of the Petén "capital." The earliest documented ruler in the inscriptions was Yax Moch Xoc, who perhaps reigned in the early 3rd century AD. A small jade plaque known as the "Leiden Plate" after the Dutch city in which it is now kept, is thought by some, though the evidence is not conclusive, to show the portrait of another famous Tikal sovereign, Bird Zero Moon. On one side of the plaque is an inscription with a date corresponding to AD 320. At the feet of the ruler depicted on the other side is a figure who seems to be a prisoner destined to be sacrificed. From this period onward, the figure of a captured enemy became a constant feature of the historical documents of Tikal, testimony to the increased power of the city state over its rivals and the frequency with which it engaged in expansionist wars. The last stela of Tikal dates to AD 869, but according to many scholars its decline had already begun around AD 830, and about a century later the city was totally abandoned.

COPAN, CITY OF THE STELAE

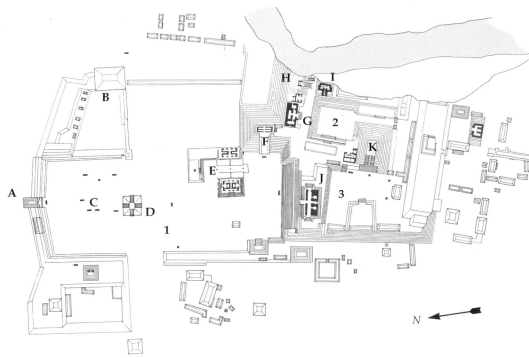

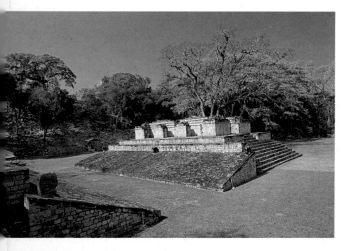

252 (top) The recently restored ball court at Copán: it has the usual capital "I" shape with the north side closed by terracing crowned with a stela.

252 (above, center) A view of the Main Plaza at Copán, scattered with commemorative stelae, altars, and terraced platforms.

252 (right, above) Numerous groups of buildings form the ceremonial center of Copán: this view shows Building 11, near the West Court.

252 (right, below) The sculpture shown here, dating from AD 762, is of a monstrous being carrying a torch in its left hand. Its iconography has been linked with the god of storms and lightning.

253 (opposite) Sculpture is frequently combined with architecture at Copán. This mask was placed as a decorative element on the Stairway of the Jaguars in the East Court.

Not far from the basin of the Motagua, along which runs the border between Guatemala and Honduras, two ceremonial centers developed during the Classic Period, Quiriguá and Copán. These two sites were linked to one another by several historical events. Both cities are rich in stelae and altars erected to celebrate the warring enterprises of their kings.

In AD 738, a king of Copán, named 18 Rabbit, was captured by the city of Quiriguá and beheaded. This marks a dramatic moment for the political and military prestige of the city of Copán, which at that time was enjoying a particularly splendid period and must have been one of the most important and populous Maya cities. Visiting the ruins of Copán today, one can still gain a sense of its cultural and economic wealth in the middle of the Classic Period, between the 5th and 9th centuries AD.

Copán was founded in a fertile hilly region watered by the Copán river, a tributary of the Motagua. Its ceremonial center covered an area of about 16 hectares (40 acres), oriented on a north–south axis and laid out in an organized way. Much of this area was occupied by platforms and man-made terraces. One of the monuments built while Copán was at its peak was the Hieroglyphic Stairway, which led to the summit of one of Copán's many imposing pyramids. This entire staircase, of 63 monolithic steps, can be "read" as a historical document as it is covered with 2,500 carved glyphs forming a lengthy inscription that lists the members of the ruling dynasty and a series of historical events. Unfortunately the inscription is badly eroded, and some details are lost. The period covered by the surviving texts stretches from AD 545 to 745.

254 The sculptors of Copán were highly accomplished, as shown by this stone head.

255/258 An impression of how Copán must have looked at its zenith: the ceremonial center, dominated by tall pyramids, was surrounded by a multitude of houses, constructed on low earth mounds in the middle of cultivated and irrigated fields. The Main Plaza was subdivided into various sections by the different monuments, while to the south rose the imposing bulk of the Acropolis.

259 A stone head found at Copán, perhaps a portrait of one of the 16 kings who succeeded one another as rulers of the city. The headdress and ear discs indicate the high rank.

UXMAL, A MASTERPIECE OF ARCHITECTURAL BALANCE

A North Group
B Terrace of
   the Monuments
C Nunnery
   Quadrangle
D Pyramid of
   the Magician
E Cemetery Group
F Ball Court

G House of the Turtles
H Palace of the
   Governor
I House of the
   Pigeons
J Great Pyramid
K South Group
L Pyramid of the
   Old Woman

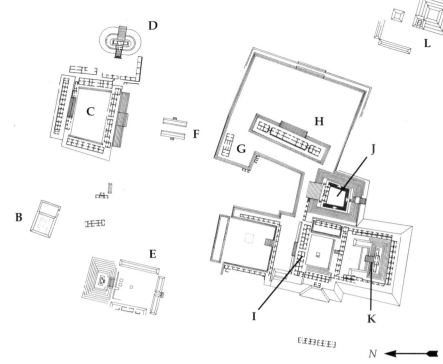

N

Uxmal is regarded as one of the masterpieces of Maya architecture, yet little has been discovered about its origins. It reached its peak during the late Classic Period when many of the central lowlands sites had already begun to decline. While the powerful Maya city states such as Palenque, Tikal, Copán, and many others were gradually abandoned and were buried by the rapid advance of tropical vegetation, other centers flourished in northern Yucatán, in an area of low hills, the Puuc. Among these centers were Uxmal, Kabah, Labná, Sayil, and Chacmultún. Archaeological investigation has confirmed their existence as early as the Preclassic Period, but it was not until many centuries later, between AD 800 and 1000, that they began to develop into important centers. The architecture of these cities developed new sophisticated and elegant forms, known as the Puuc style after the name of the region.

Uxmal is perhaps the center that achieved the greatest political and economic development in the Puuc area and today it is the best preserved archaeological site. Many stelae stand on the Terrace of the Monuments, but they have provided little historical information. One fact recorded is the name of a king Chac, who ruled the city in around AD 900.

The decorative richness of the Puuc style reached its peak at Uxmal and the remains of the ceremonial center are stunning testimony to a world completely different from that of the grand and severe jungle cities. One typical feature of the Puuc style was the use of stone mosaics that covered the upper façades of the buildings

262 (opposite above left) Two of Uxmal's most important buildings: the Palace of the Governor and, immediately behind, the Great Pyramid.

262 (opposite above right) Part of the complex known as "The House of the Pigeons." Its name derives from the roofcombs which resemble dovecotes.

262–263 (left) Uxmal's buildings emerge from the forest vegetation: on the right is the Pyramid of the Magician, unique for its oval plan, and on the left can be seen the upper section of the Nunnery Quadrangle, the internal courtyard of which resembles a convent.

263 (below) The façade of the House of the Turtles is characterized by a sober and elegant architectural style. The building owes its name to the turtle sculptures over the columned frieze above the three doors.

with motifs such as frets, lozenges, stylized animals, and half-columns forming friezes similar to elaborate textiles. Monster masks in stone and stucco relating to the god Chac indicate the importance of this religious cult.

Ceilings created using the corbeling technique and cylindrical columns with square capitals are other characteristic elements of the buildings of the period. Some of the friezes decorating the Puuc-style buildings of Uxmal, such as the Nunnery Quadrangle, incorporate a motif showing a stylized version of the traditional Maya hut with a thatched roof. This, together with depictions on the Arch of Labná and the murals at Chichén Itzá are our only evidence of ordinary Maya houses.

The architectural complexes at Uxmal generally have an elongated rectangular plan with numerous rooms set around plazas and large courtyards, hence the term quadrangle is often used. While they are generally considered to be royal palaces and ceremonial buildings, their original function is uncertain. Among the most famous are undoubtedly the House of the Turtles, the Nunnery Quadrangle—which is so called because of its resemblance to a convent, with numerous cells arranged around a large internal courtyard—and the Palace of the Governor built on a massive platform incorporating structures from earlier periods. Archaeologists have established that rather than being casually positioned, the palace was carefully oriented: from the central doorway astronomers could observe

264 (opposite above left) In front of the Pyramid of the Magician is a courtyard closed on three sides by a low portico. A gateway opens to the Nunnery Quadrangle.

264 (opposite above right) This striking monument represents a two-headed feline and has been called "The Altar of the Jaguars." It may have acted as an altar on which men and animals were sacrificed. In the background is the Palace of the Governor.

264–265 The imposing bulk of the Pyramid of the Magician illuminated by the setting sun.

265 (above) Part of the decoration of the Pyramid of the Magician, this sculpture depicts a figure, perhaps a deity or a ruler of Uxmal, emerging from the jaws of a serpent.

the planet Venus on the horizon as it climbed through the sky to the tip of a pyramid situated several miles away. Here again we should reflect that so many buildings to which we give simple names, such as "palace" or "temple," in reality probably had far more complex functions.

In Uxmal there are also pyramid complexes and a court for the ritual ball game, both part of the Classic Period Maya cultural tradition. But the most extraordinary temple is undoubtedly the great pyramid with an oval base, the only one of its kind, known as the Pyramid of the Magician. Composed of a number of superimposed structures, the building has a stairway on the south-west side that leads up to a small sanctuary. The external façade of this is decorated in the Chenes style, depicting a monster mask with gaping jaws. A row of masks of the god Chac with prominent noses, positioned along the sides of the stairway, once again indicate the importance of the cult of this god.

At the top of the pyramid is another large sanctuary added in a later phase and built in the style typical of the Campeche region. This could be reached via a second staircase climbing up the eastern side. Recent restoration work has cleared the base of the pyramid to reveal the remains of a long colonnade that probably once surrounded the entire structure.

Several other fine buildings at Uxmal demonstrate a blending of styles from different regions and can be dated to the various phases of the city's development. One example is the House of the Pigeons, perhaps a palace, that is possibly older than the other buildings discussed above. Like many of the buildings at Uxmal it is crowned by a pierced roofcomb that

resembles the dovecotes of European architecture. The walls of the House of the Pigeons still retain traces of stucco decorative elements.

In the Cemetery Group blocks carved in low relief include motifs of the skull and crossbones, inevitably recalling the *tzompantli* of Chichén Itzá, and are presumably features of Toltec origin.

266–267 The Nunnery Quadrangle is one of Uxmal's most celebrated architectural complexes. The first European travelers to visit these ruins gave the building the name still in use today, as they thought the vast complex composed of small rooms around the internal courtyard resembles the structure of a convent. In fact we still do not know the function of the four separate large buildings that form this complex.

267 (above) This decorative element, a detail from the West Palace, part of the Nunnery Quadrangle, perhaps epitomises the elegance of the Puuc style. Set against a finely cut stone mosaic consisting of geometric motifs, a relief sculpture depicts the Feathered Serpent with a human head emerging from its jaws.

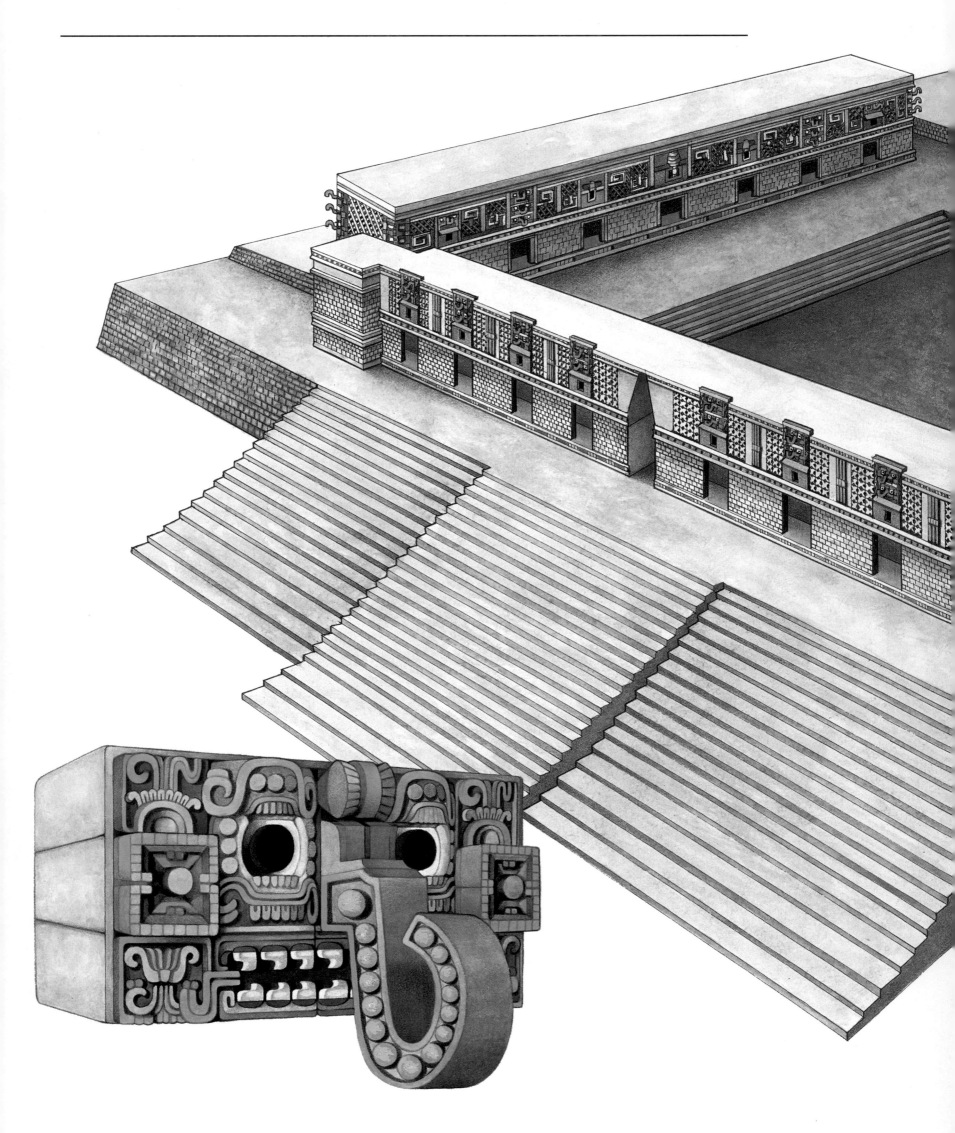

268 (left) Almost all the brilliant painted decoration that embellished buildings of the Maya world has disappeared: this drawing, reproducing one of the masks of Chac repeated in the façade of the Nunnery Quadrangle, helps to give an idea of the original impact of these buildings.

268–269 The Nunnery Quadrangle is restored to its original appearance in this reconstruction. It was composed of four separate buildings overlooking a rectangular courtyard measuring 45 m (147 ft) by 65 m (213 ft) and built on a platform. The complex was reached by a long stairway in three sections, that led to a majestic gateway communicating with the courtyard. Inside each of the four buildings were two parallel rows of non-communicating rooms. The façades were decorated with geometric friezes and large masks of the god Chac.

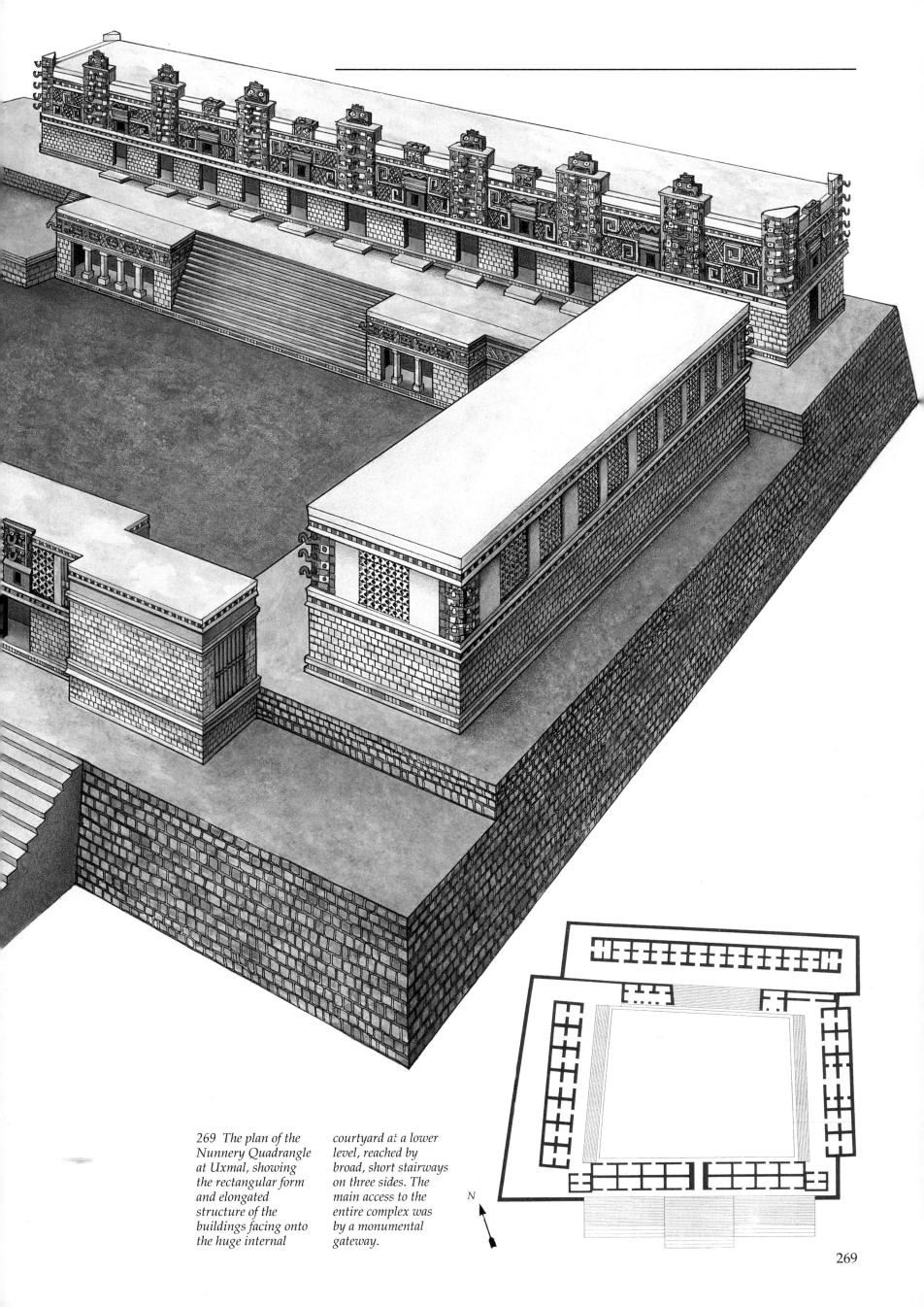

269 The plan of the Nunnery Quadrangle at Uxmal, showing the rectangular form and elongated structure of the buildings facing onto the huge internal courtyard at a lower level, reached by broad, short stairways on three sides. The main access to the entire complex was by a monumental gateway.

N

270 (right) The rear of the Palace of the Masks, or Codz Poop, at Kabah. This rectangular structure, crowned by a prominent roofcomb, dates to the 9th century AD and was built on a low platform.

270–271 The Palace of the Masks at Kabah is named after the 260 identical monster masks representing the god Chac which cover its principal façade. In the plaza in front of the building are the remains of a wall covered with relief glyphs.

271 (opposite below) This statue is carved on the rear façade of the Codz Poop. Its rigid severity is very reminiscent of the art of the Huaxtecs and Aztecs.

KABAH, THE VENERATION OF CHAC

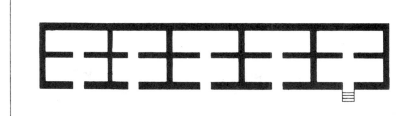

Plan of the Codz Poop   N ←

271 (center) This detail of the Palace of the Masks shows how the entire façade is covered with large masks of Chac, the god of rain and fertility.

271 (bottom) The internal corridors of the Palace of the Masks were roofed by corbeled ceilings.

Excavations and restorations recently completed at Kabah, not far from Sayil and Labná, have brought to light interesting architectural features about which little was previously known. The most extraordinary and eye-catching building of this ancient city is the Codz Poop, also known as the Palace of the Masks, which dates to the 9th century AD.

The unusual element of this wonderful building is its main façade, which is completely covered with masks depicting Chac, the god of rain and fertility. Although the iconography of this god recurs in the architecture of the Puuc-style centers, in the palace of Kabah it seems to attain even greater importance and perhaps greater strength in this seemingly obsessive repetition.

The building, rectangular in plan, is 45 m (147 ft) long and is crowned with a fine roofcomb. It was originally covered with 260 identical masks with their characteristic feature of a prominent nose. Typically the number of masks was not simply random— 260 is also the number of days in the Maya Ritual Calendar known as *tzolkin*. Here too, as in the majority of the ancient Maya cities, we see a clear indication of the importance of the computation of time.

Inside the palace, between one room and another is a kind of "step" which is in fact composed of the rolled up proboscis of Chac—the name Codz Poop means "Rolled Mat." This element recalls the special mats that were unrolled and laid out for dignitaries to sit or walk on and suggests that access to the internal rooms was restricted to high ranking figures, but the issue is still debated.

On the east side of the Palace of the Masks is another building excavated

and restored in the 1990s, the importance of which is linked to the presence of a series of statues that are very unusual in Puuc architecture. They depict standing male figures with extremely rigid postures that some specialists have described as "robotic." Their mustaches, crowns, and skin scarifications confirm that they were members of the ruling caste.

Kabah is also noteworthy for another structure that has become very famous—a monumental freestanding arch stands on a terrace at the end of the causeway, or *sacbe*, that links Kabah and Uxmal. Kabah's Great Arch was perhaps built simply to endow the city center with a monumental entrance, or to mark a border between the outer, profane area of the town and the inner, sacred one. Architecturally the monument is extremely simple: it was constructed using the corbeling technique and lacks the elaborate relief decorations that embellish the arch of Labná.

272–273 The buildings of Kabah in the Yucatán reveal the sober elegance of Puuc-style architecture that developed toward the end of the Classic Period. These are the remains of one of the palaces of the city facing onto a square of large dimensions. The building, with a rectangular structure, is composed of two stories and is topped by a low roof comb. The lower floor is subdivided into small rooms, each with a doorway resembling those of the Nunnery Quadrangle at Uxmal. A flight of steps leads to the upper story, with a long internal corridor.

272 (opposite below) This large plaza represents the heart of the city of Kabah. The base of a rectangular structure with columns is visible; in the background are the ruins of a pyramidal building still littered with rubble and, on the right, is the rear facade of the Codz Poop.

273 The Great Arch of Kabah, a monumental gateway at the southern end of the road linking Kabah with Uxmal. Although it lacks the decoration that is such a feature of the Arch of Labná, this is a magnificent example of the corbeled vault typical of the Puuc cities of the late Classic Period.

LABNA,
A PUUC-STYLE JEWEL

Together with Sayil and Uxmal, the city of Labná is one of the most important examples of the Puuc architectural style. Today, what immediately catches the eye of visitors to the ancient site is undoubtedly the monumental arch that rises at the foot of a religious pyramidal building known as the "Castillo." Despite a superficial similarity in form to the triumphal arches of the Roman Empire, this gateway was in fact a covered passage between two irregular monumental complexes, mostly reduced to ruins today.

The arch is flanked by two roughly square rooms communicating with the outside by two doors facing west. It was built using the corbeling technique, and its elegance is accentuated by the decorations on its upper surfaces, which are different on each façade. On the western side, against a background of lozenges, are two elements in low relief depicting a form of simple hut with a thatched roof. Originally there were probably two statues in the niches that represent the doorways of the huts. On the left corner is a mask, the prominent nose of which recalls the iconography of Chac, who was still worshiped in the era of the Spanish Conquest. A similar monster mask and decorations in the Puuc style can also be seen in the ruins of what was probably a ceremonial building of considerable size, known as the "Palace."

On the other side of the arch the decoration consists of a frieze of geometric motifs set against a background of half-columns. Finally, the whole monument, was surmounted by a crest with regular rectangular openings.

274 (opposite left, above) In the background is the sacbe, or causeway, leading to the Palace of Labná.

274 (opposite left, below) The Arch of Labná overlooks a courtyard at the center of which stand the remains of an altar.

274–275 (below) It is thought that the arch, the rear of which is shown here, originally acted as a covered passage linking two groups of buildings.

275 (left) The "Mirador" is so-named because of its elevated position overlooking the rest of the site. The pyramidal platform on which the temple stands is still today strewn with rubble.

EDZNA, A MEETING OF DIVERSE STYLES

280 (below) This view of the site of Edzná is from the building known as the Nohol Na: in the background on the left rises the Five-Story Palace.

280–281 (right) The Five-Story Palace can be considered as a hybrid between the ancient Maya pyramidal structure and the Puuc-style palaces; the temple at the summit is topped by a roofcomb.

The city of Edzná, located in an isolated valley in the Campeche region, on the border between the Puuc and Chenes areas, reached its peak in the late Classic Period, in the 8th and 9th centuries AD. Although it was influenced by the architectural styles of neighboring regions, it developed an autonomous culture that some experts have defined as a hybrid or a transitional phase between the Puuc style—evident in the use of monolithic columns—that of Chenes, and that of Río Bec.

Edzná was probably an independent kingdom until the end of the Classic Period when it sank into a rapid decline and was abandoned, like

281 (opposite below left) The fifth story of the Palace of Edzná is occupied by a simple temple structure, the interior of which is reached by a doorway preceded by four massive pilasters. The remains of the roofcomb can be seen in the upper section.

many other Maya cities. Various stone stelae found in the ceremonial center carry inscriptions dating to the political and cultural zenith of the city. It is presumed that, at its cultural height, a ruling dynasty exercised power not only over the urban center, but also over the rural population of the surrounding valley, where a massive system of canals that was laid out and constructed in the Late Preclassic period may still have been in use.

In its layout, the ceremonial center of Edzná recalls that of Tikal and other cities that developed in earlier ages in the Petén region. Edzná's main nucleus is grouped around a rectangular plaza, where traces of ancient stucco decorations are still visible. The open space is inclined toward the south to allow rain water to run off. It is on this side of the square that the most important complex of buildings rises, the so-called Great Acropolis, which has recently been extensively restored. Another building forming part of the ceremonial center is the "Nohol Na," or the Temple of Nohol, a sacred building with a very long façade. Not far from this building is a complex of buildings of various dates and known as the Temple of the Knives.

The most famous of the group of buildings comprising the Acropolis is the Five-Story Palace, dating from the Puuc period but built over an older construction. It has a pyramidal structure composed of four levels crowned by a fifth with the actual sanctuary, decorated with an impressive roofcomb 6 m (20 ft) high. This is a clear reference to the sacred buildings of Tikal. On the first story are seven rooms, the entrances to which were embellished with pilasters in the Río Bec style. The fourth story, on the other hand, features cylindrical columns in the Puuc style. A steep stairway leads up to the sanctuary. Two typical elements of the local style stand out in the architectural complex: the corbel vault and the cylindrical column, acquired by the Maya only toward the end of the Classic Period, but used by other Mesoamerican peoples many centuries earlier. Based on the arrangement of internal rooms, some scholars consider the "Five-Story Palace" to be a hybrid of a palace and a pyramid.

281 (opposite below right) The North Temple on the great Acropolis has a very massive structure, like the others at Edzná, but it is less elegant than the Five-Story Palace.

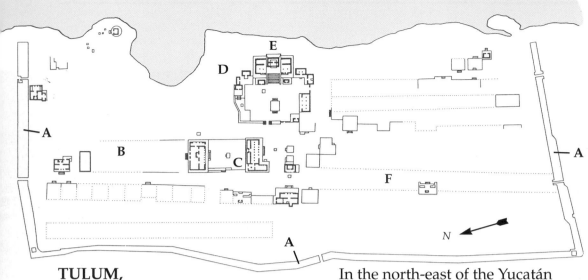

TULUM, THE FORTRESS BY THE SEA

A Walls
B Market
C Palace

D Temple of the Frescoes
E Castillo
F Principal road

In the north-east of the Yucatán peninsula, in a spectacular setting at the top of a cliff, is Tulum, an important port and trading center. It is also one of the last Maya outposts of the late Post-Classic Period. Built in AD 1200, it reached the peak of its development two centuries later, following the decline of the city of Mayapán. Like other centers around the coast in the same period, Tulum was surrounded by defensive walls, here on three sides, with watchtowers and walkways. A number of roads linked the urban center of Tulum with the forests of the interior.

In 1518, when the Spanish Conquistadores led by Juan de Grijalva arrived, the city was still inhabited and the sanctuary dedicated to the goddess Ixchel on the nearby island of Cozumel was still a destination for pilgrims. Some time after the Conquest, the site was abandoned and forgotten until 1841, the year in which it was explored by the celebrated travelers John Stephens and Frederick Catherwood.

At Tulum, as at other coastal centers, there is a clear blending of architectural elements of Maya and Mexican origin. One of the main buildings, and probably one of the oldest in the city, is the so-called "Castillo," built above a sheer drop to the sea. A colonnade here is a clear indication of the Maya-Toltec influence from Chichén Itzá. The second notable building, the Temple of the Frescoes, dates from the late Post-Classic Period. Its interior walls are decorated with wall paintings in blue, red, and yellow. Their subject matter is mythological, centered on a mysterious deity known as the "Descending God." These frescoes are very reminiscent of the style of the paintings found in the codices produced by the Mixtecs of Oaxaca.

284 (top) The Temple of the Frescoes at Tulum is perhaps one of the last monuments constructed by the Maya people before the Spanish Conquest.

284 (center) The largest building in Tulum is the Castillo, located in a dramatic position on a cliff-top overlooking the sea.

284–285 (right) This panoramic view of the remains of Tulum may give some idea of the impression experienced by the Spanish navigators who saw the citadel perched on the cliff-top. Tulum rose to power after the fall of Mayapán and was still inhabited in the 16th century when the Europeans arrived.

285 (opposite below left) A detail of the summit of the Castillo of Tulum. The structure has some characteristics of a fortified site.

285 (opposite below right) The so-called "Palace" has an elongated plan and a colonnaded atrium.

286–287 Tulum, in its enchanting setting, was both a trading center and and a fortified citadel.

292 *This clay whistle of Maya origin from Jainá Island depicts a maracas player.*

292